AWFUL
ART

D0111210

The Knowledge

AWFUL ART

BY MICHAEL COX

ILLUSTRATED BY PHILIP REEVE

Hippo

Scholastic Children's Books,
Commonwealth House, 1–19 New Oxford Street,
London WC1A 1NU, UK
A division of Scholastic Ltd
London ~ New York ~ Toronto ~ Sydney ~ Auckland
Mexxico City ~ New Delhi ~ Hong Kong

Published in the UK by Scholastic Ltd, 1997
Text copyright © Michael Cox, 1997
Illustrations copyright © Philip Reeve, 1997

All rights reserved

ISBN 0 590 19262 0

Typeset by TW Typesetting, Midsomer Norton, Avon
Printed and bound by Nørhaven Paperback A/S, Denmark

16 18 20 19 17

The right of Michael Cox and Philip Reeve to be identified as the
author and illustrator of this work respectively has been asserted by
them in accordance with the Copyright, Designs and Patents Act, 1988.

Contents

Michael Cox wanted to be Van Gogh when he was young, but his teacher told him it wasn't possible – he had too many ears. Michael's grown up now, and when he's not jetting off on exciting, all expenses paid fact-finding missions to the local library, he spends his  time at home in Nottinghamshire with his six chickens, two cats and some grown ups who claim to be his family. As well as writing books, he teaches, and paints pictures of things like sheep and trees.

Philip Reeve used to make home made science fiction blockbuster movies until his friends got fed up of running round in cardboard hats. He thought that illustrating books would be easier, and he's been illustrating now for two years. He lives in Brighton, and in his spare  time he writes books that nobody wants to read and plays that nobody wants to see. His ambitions for the future include writing books that people *do* want to read and plays that people *do* want to see.

INTRODUCTION

Have you ever looked at those awful multi-coloured splodges on your teacher's tie and asked yourself...

Is that an exciting art design based on the paintings of Jackson Pollock, the famous action painter ... or is my teacher just a messy eater?

Art is awful, isn't it? At times it can be confusing, infuriating, baffling, scary and ... well ... incredibly weird! Occasionally, it's also absolutely disgusting (so don't read this book if you are easily shocked, or are a grown-up). On the other hand it's nearly always tons of fun, awfully exciting and awfully interesting!

In a recent survey, quite a few out of ten school children expressed a preference for art over several other well known brands of classroom torture. And, in a discussion about art, those same children said that they wished they knew more about this fascinating subject. Some of them even asked exciting and lively questions like, "Who were the first ever artists? What's art for? How can you tell if something is real art? What are artists actually like?" and "Can we go for our lunch yet?"

One or two admitted that they had embarrassing gaps in their knowledge of art history...

This book will answer questions like these. It will also tell you a few other awfully interesting things about art that you probably didn't know, like ...

- **how** the world famous artist, Pablo Picasso, was let down by a sausage.
- **why** the sculptor, Joseph Nollekins, hardly ever changed his underpants.
- **what** the artist, Mark Quinn, did with nine pints of his own blood and ...
- **where** the painter, A. L. Girodet, stuck his candles while he was painting.

It may help you to discover whether or not you are the right sort of person to become an artist ... and show you why some artists rocket to fame and fortune while others plummet to pain and poverty.

If we'd tried to tell you ALL of the awfully interesting things that there are to know about art

8

this book would have been at least as big as a multi-storey car park – and we probably wouldn't have been able to fit it through the bookshop door. So we've had to leave out a few thousand stories but we've still managed to include:

- fascinating facts about the art that is so incredibly old and ancient that even your headteacher won't remember it!
- things about the art that is so new (and weird!) that the people who read the news on T.V. probably don't even know about it
- stories about the artists whose work was so nightmarish and shocking it caused a riot
- terrific tales of foxy fraudsters, fab finds, doomed daubers, jammy bodgers and genuine geniuses
- … an interview with an apple!

So – if you want to find out which artist liked to use toilet rolls as sketch pads, which one dyed his hair with boot polish and which one wanted to put dynamite in a duck's bottom – read on!

Hopefully, you'll find it all awfully interesting!

HOW ART GOT OFF TO A TERRIFYING START

Place: A cave somewhere in France
Time: Fifteen thousand years ago

Pa Homo-sapiens burped noisily then wiped his hands on the corner of Ma Homo-sapiens' bison fur mini-skirt.

"Mmmm, that was a delicious bit of mammoth, my dear," he said. "So succulent, so tender! You can't beat the free-range variety is what I say. It takes a bit of persuading to get them to fall off the edge of the cliff, but it's well worth it in the end!"

"But dad!" protested Arthur Homo-sapiens, the youngest and smartest of Ma and Pa Homo-sapiens' 23 children, "all mammoths are free-range! They wander wherever they choose. That's why we have to hunt them at such great risk to our personal safety."

"Is it?" said Pa Homo-sapiens, scratching his gorilla-like cranium in confusion.

"Of course it is!" said Arthur, who was generally considered to be something of a useless wimp by the rest of the family. He paused, then added thoughtfully, "Though I'm sure a time will come when there will be mammoth farms and pre-packed select cuts of mammoth steak readily available at specialist outlets ... but not in our lifetime, Dad."

Pa Homo-sapiens' overhanging eyebrows jutted out even further above his overhanging eyes as he listened to his remarkably clever son.

"I'd never thought of that," he said, and bit the head off the giant cave louse which had just crawled out of his hairy chest.

"That's because your brain's not as big as mine," said Arthur. "I am your son and therefore I am further up the evolutionary tree than you are."

"We're not up a tree … we're in a cave!" said Pa Homo-sapiens, feeling even more confused.

"What a Neolithic ninny!" said Arthur, under his smelly breath.

"Don't you be so cheeky to your father! You little know-it-all Neanderthal!" snapped Ma Homo-sapiens and she gave Arthur a mighty wallop with the thigh-bone of a giant reindeer. "You're getting too big for your hippo-skin moccasins, you are! Just for that you can tidy away the dinner things while the rest of us settle down to a pleasant evening staring at the fire."

The rest of the Homo-sapiens clan moved away from the dining area and gathered around the fire, leaving Arthur to clear up the mess. In no time at all they were completely engrossed in that evening's flickerings, clapping and grunting appreciatively

11

whenever they thought they spotted a familiar face in the flames.

Meanwhile in the far corner of the cave, Arthur, being a sensitive and thoughtful boy, became bored with his tedious tidying task and started to jab and scrape angrily at the cave wall with a charred mammoth bone. He soon began to enjoy himself and realized that this was the perfect way to express his frustration at being so misunderstood and undervalued by his lowbrow family.

About half an hour passed.

"What *can* that boy be doing?" asked Ma Homo-sapiens. "Surely it can't be taking him *that* long to tidy away a few bones and a bit of mammoth gristle? I'll just go and see what he's up to."

She lumbered over to Arthur to see what could be keeping him, but as she drew near to him, she saw something that made the hairs on her back stand on end. She began to whimper with fear. Alerted by her cries of horror, the rest of the family looked in the direction of young Arthur and, moments later, they too, were cowering in a corner of the cave gibbering in terror at the awful sight that met their eyes.

Somehow, while they had all been busy watching the fire, a vast herd of woolly mammoths had snuck into their cave! The huge beasts were now cavorting and trundling around young Arthur, who sat there, completely unperturbed, spare-rib in hand!

Pa Homo-sapiens was the first to speak.

"G... g... get those creatures out of here, Ar... Arthur!" he stammered, "before they trample us to death."

"It's all right Dad, they're not real," said Arthur, "I've just made them."

"Of course they're real! I can see them!" shouted Pa Homo-sapiens. "They've got tusks and four legs

13

and all their other bits, they must be real! Someone get a spear and kill them before they get us."

Ma Homo-sapiens peered quizzically at the huge beasts and, suddenly, she realized that all was not as it seemed.

"Just a minute ... calm down, you lily-livered Cro-magnon!" she said to her quivering mate. Then, turning to her son, she asked, "All right, Art, if they're *not* real, where *did* they come from?"

"I've just told you! I made them ... with this!" said Arthur, proudly holding up the charred mammoth rib. "Look! It's easy. I'll show you."

Arthur made several deft and accomplished strokes with the blackened bone and, as if by magic, yet another cantering mammoth miraculously appeared on the cave wall. The whole family took two paces back and gasped in awe. Ma Homo-sapiens gave her husband an excited look and said, "You know what this means, don't you?"

"Yes I do!" said the still trembling Pa Homo-sapiens, "if he doesn't stop soon we're going to be up to our ears in mammoth poo!"

"No, not that, you Palaeolithic pinhead!" said Ma. "It's our son, our Art. He's got magic powers. He can magic mammoths out of thin air. Just like that!"

With an expression of respect and wonder on her craggy face, she smiled at her grinning son, and said, "Can you do woolly rhinoceroses as well, Art?"

"I'm not sure, Mum," said Arthur, "but I'll have a go."

Arthur's talent for making animals seem to gallop across the cave walls came on in leaps and bounds.

14

He even learned to colour in his creations, making them look more lifelike and scary than ever!

The elders of the tribe were so impressed with his magic skills that they decided to give him a cave of his own where he could conjure up bears and bison and woolly mammoths to his heart's content. In no time at all, this cave, which was known as Art's gallery, became filled with terrifying and beautiful images of the tasty, but often ferocious creatures that the Homo-sapiens tribe depended on for their survival.

News of Art's tremendous talent spread far and wide. Stone-Age mums and dads began to take their children to visit the gallery so that they could admire his creations and learn something about the savage beasts that they would one day have to engage in hand to hoof combat – and (*hopefully*) knock the stuffing out of. As the Neanderthal nippers gazed in awe-struck wonder at the pictures, their parents would say, "These are the wonderful works of Art – aren't they beautiful? Art has got special powers and must always be treated with great reverence!"

So that is how Art came to be respected and to play an important and useful role in Prehistoric society.

Robot's big adventure

PLACE - THE SAME BIT OF FRANCE. TIME - FIFTEEN THOUSAND YEARS LATER... SEPTEMBER 1940

FOUR BOYS WERE HUNTING FOR RABBITS WITH THEIR DOG, WHOSE NAME WAS **ROBOT**, WHEN...

QUELLE HORREUR! MY LITTLE ROBOT 'AS DISAPPEARED *

ROBOT HAD FALLEN THROUGH A SMALL CRACK IN THE EARTH KNOWN AS **THE DEVIL'S HOLE**...

'E AS GONE DOWN ZAT LITTLE 'OLE I CAN 'EAR 'IM BARKING!

LET US GO DOWN ZE 'OLE

LE WOOF!

THE HOLE WAS MADE 12 YEARS EARLIER WHEN A LARGE TREE WAS WRENCHED FROM THE EARTH BY A STORM. IT WAS TOO NARROW FOR THE BOYS TO ENTER...

IT EEZ TOO SMALL. WE WILL GET STURK!

DON'T WORRY I 'AVE MY SCOUT KNIFE WIZ ME. I WILL MAKE IT BIGGUR IN NO TIME!

WHAT - ZE KNIFE?

NO, ZE 'OLE, YOU NURM-SKULL!

THE FIRST BOY, WHOSE NAME WAS **RAVIDAT**, DUG AWAY AT THE HOLE WITH HIS KNIFE. WHEN THE GAP WAS BIG ENOUGH HE SQUEEZED THROUGH...

* IN ORDER TO GIVE A FEELING OF AUTHENTICITY. THE SPOKEN BITS ARE IN THE ORIGINAL FRENCH. YOU MAY NEED A TRANSLATOR...

16

HE FOUND HIMSELF IN A HUGE, DARK UNDERGROUND CHAMBER – AND SOMETHING WET AND SLIMY WAS CRAWLING UP THE BACK OF HIS HAND!

UURGH! WHAT EEZ ZAT?

WUFF! WUFF!

ZOOT ALORS! EET EEZ A LITTLE DOGGY TONGUE LICKING MY 'AND! EET EEZ MY ROBOT! VOILA, 'E EEZ SAFE! COME ON DOWN BOYS... OR ARE YOU A FLURK OF CHEEKURNS?

WUFF!

THE OTHER BOYS SCRAMBLED DOWN THE HOLE...

QUELLE SURPRISE! EET EEZ WELL WICKED DOWN 'ERE!

BUT EET EEZ SO DURK! I FEEL A BIT FRATTENED

ME TOO! LET'S GO 'OME AND GET A LERMP!

THE BOYS WENT HOME AND RETURNED TO THE HOLE A FEW DAYS LATER. THIS TIME THEY BROUGHT AN OIL LAMP

TOUT ALORS!

EET EEZ AMAZZING!

THE WALLS OF THE CAVE WERE COVERED WITH PAINTINGS OF ANIMALS. SOME OF THEM WERE ENORMOUS. ONE OF THE BULLS WAS 17 FEET LONG!

ZEY ARE BEAUTIFUL! BUT WHEN WERE ZEY PAINTED?

WOOF! WUFF! GRRRRR!

I DON'T KNOW– BUT I KNOW 'OO WILL! MONSIEUR LAVAL, OUR SCHOOL TEACHER! WE WILL GO AN' GET 'IM!

Lascaux fact file

1 The people who saw the pictures in the caves at Lascaux found them so awe inspiring and spooky that they called them the Eighth Wonder of the World.

2 When the boys first found them, the paintings probably looked as fresh and clear as the day they'd been painted. This was because the original entrance to the cave (the one that had been used by the prehistoric artists) had been blocked by a rock fall and the paintings were perfectly protected from damp and extreme changes in temperature by the thick rock of the cave roof. They were also covered by a layer of crystals – this had the same effect as sealing them under a huge sheet of cling-film.

3 A few years after the boys' amazing discovery, an artificial entrance was made to the Lascaux caves and electric lighting was put in. Ravidat and his pals, who were all young men by now, were employed as guides for the thousands of people who came to see the pictures.

4 The caves became so famous that, quite soon, 2,000 people a day were visiting them ... then ... disaster

18

struck! After being perfectly preserved for at least 14,000 years, the pictures began to fade! Experts soon realized that the breath of the visitors and the changes in light and temperature were causing the Eighth Wonder of the World to disappear before their very eyes! Something drastic had to be done very quickly. But what? Which of the following solutions to the problem would you have chosen?

a) Switch off all of the lights and ask the visitors to hold their breath and imagine the paintings.
b) Make an exact life size replica of the whole cave and let the public visit that instead.
c) Close the caves down permanently and show visitors a book of snapshots.

Answer: b). Art enthusiasts from all over the world were so disappointed by the closure of the caves that it was decided to make an exact copy of them (the caves *not* the art lovers) using computer calculations and modern materials. An underground replica was built using steel girders, wire mesh, breeze blocks and concrete. The interior of the whole

19

structure was covered in clay and modelled by sculptors so that the exact shape of the original caves was reproduced down to the nearest few square inches. Pictorial artists were then employed to paint in the animals. Wherever they could, they used the Stone Age pigments (colours) that had been found nearby. The fake Lascaux caves were opened to the public in 1983. People who knew the original Lascaux were astonished. They said that going into the copy was just like going into the genuine thing for the first time. You could say that it was the biggest, most ambitious and most successful forgery of a work of art in the whole world. It is visited by a third of a million people a year and is so popular that if you wish to see it during the summer you have to book months in advance.

Prehistoric arty-facts

1 There is prehistoric art and ancient art all over the world. Human beings seem to have been making art since they could hold a charred bit of wood or bone, or hack out a design on a reindeer's antler (assuming it wasn't still attached to the reindeer).

2 There are many genuine cave paintings to be seen in southern France and Spain and, no doubt, there are still many more waiting to be discovered by pot-holing dogs. Sadly there are probably even more that will never be found because the caves which they are in have been filled by falls of earth and rock.

3 In one cave, quite near Lascaux, there are about

120 paintings of mammoths (perhaps this is the cave in our first story?). It is called The Cave of the Mammoths and is so far under the ground that an electric railway system has been built to transport the visitors to it. The original artists made their own way to the remote chambers along miles of underground tunnels (because they'd got really fed up waiting for the train?). In order to see in the dark they used lamps made from moss soaked in animal fat (or ate lots of carrots). Whenever they were faced with the descent of difficult and dangerous shafts they used ladders made from grass and creepers (or just fell down them). The whole experience was no doubt extremely scary and risky, especially as savage bears hibernated in the caves during the winter.

4 The Cave of the Mammoths has been known about and explored since the 15th century and, ever since then, graffiti artists from other ages have left their own doodlings and messages on top of the original cave paintings.

21

5 In the Tarn Valley in southern France, boy scouts were employed in a local "clean up graffiti campaign". The boy scouts were a bit too thorough and conscientious in their work. They scrubbed away everything they could find – including two rare and priceless prehistoric wall paintings of bison that had been created 15,000 years earlier.

6 Many of the caves have handprints and hand silhouettes on the walls next to the paintings. The cave artists couldn't read or write so it is thought that the hand prints might have been their way of signing their work. In one cave there are prints on the wall which have been made by someone's bottom. No one is quite sure what this artist was trying to say! It could have been a message to ... posteriority?

7 The cave paintings at Altamira in Spain were also discovered when a dog (no, not Robot, *another* dog – it was in 1830) went down a hole. This dog had chased a fox into a network of caves. Its owner followed it along an underground passage accompanied by his five-year-old daughter. The ceiling of the underground passage was very low, so the man had to keep his head bowed, but the little girl was able to look up. She was astonished to see that the ceiling was covered with paintings of what she first thought were bulls, but were later identified as prehistoric bison.

People didn't believe the man when he told them about the pictures and a local professor accused him of employing an artist to fake the paintings. The pictures were eventually found to have been created thousands of years earlier – the experts aren't *always* right.

8 Prehistoric artists didn't just make cave pictures. They were sculptors as well. Archaeologists have discovered small carvings of bison, mammoths and human figures.

9 One of the biggest mysteries in prehistoric art are the giant rocks known as Stonehenge. Some experts believe these rocks were once the site of pagan festivals held by very primitive people (or raves – as we now know them).

Make your own cave paintings

Before you can produce successful cave art you must get into the right frame of mind. This is called, "getting into character". Actors do it all the time. Your task is to wipe away 20,000 years of evolution and civilization in just a few days. You must assume the habits and personality of a Neolithic hunter. (No doubt this will be extremely easy for some of you.)

Getting primitive – some handy tips

1 Do not wash or eat for at least three days. Get into the habit of wearing animal skins (first check that they do not already contain an animal).

2 Practise dragging your knuckles on the pavement as you walk to school, gibber at passing motor cars and sniff passers-by suspiciously.

3 Pretend you don't understand a thing your teacher says (what do you mean, "What's new?").

4 Do not sit at your desk in class – sit on a shelf or on top of a cupboard. If your teacher reprimands you, don't sulk, just curl back your top lip and snarl menacingly.

5 Offer to search your friend's pelt for vermin during

morning playtime...

6 Sleep under your bed, not in it – offer fruit to the T.V. newsreader – stalk the milkman.

Feeling Palaeolithic? Good. You must now find a site for your painting. Obviously a cave would be perfect but if you haven't got one, the following substitutes are acceptable:

a) a cellar

b) a disused dog kennel (keep a look out for the disused dog!)

c) a garden shed.

If none of these are available why not just find an old piece of wood and cover it in hypertufa? Hyperwhat? Read on and find out!

ACTIVITY

Getting down to the nitty gritty – how to make hypertufa

You can use hypertufa to make a cave wall surface on a piece of roughened hardboard or thin plywood.

What you'll need:

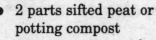

- 2 parts sifted peat or potting compost
- 2 parts coarse sand
- 2 parts cement
- 1 part P.V.A. glue
- water
- an old spoon or stick for mixing
- a bucket or plastic container

a paint scraper or
builder's trowel

All you have to do
- Mix the peat, sand and
cement and P.V.A. glue
with enough water to
make a thick paste.

SERIOUS WARNING – WEAR STRONG RUBBER GLOVES WHEN HANDLING THE PASTE!

- Spread the paste over the
board with your hands,
to a depth of about two
centimetres.
- Shape the surface until it
resembles your favourite
bit of cave wall. Leave to
dry!
- Then, when you are
completely dry, return to
your hypertufa. If it is still
wet go and organize your…

Painting materials
The cave people had to experiment to find materials.
They often discovered them by accident … like Art's
charred bone. He might just as easily have used a
bit of burnt wood (charcoal) to sketch his animals, or
a bit of calcium carbonate (chalk).

If you are not feeling too adventurous you can use
ordinary painting materials, but remember, you

must only use reds, browns, yellows and blacks, to give your Art-work that authentic cave painting look. If you wish to experiment with natural materials, just like Art did, ask an adult to help you (preferably a Neanderthal type ... e.g. a teacher) and – BE SAFE!

Pigments
When Art was looking for colours he probably dug most of them from the ground. They'd probably be the bits of rock he found most colourful. These are your "pigments". When you've found some attractively coloured bits of rock you have to grind them into a powder (do *not* use the family food processor).

The number of colours available to Art was quite limited. In order to add new colours to his palette he heated some of them up until they took on a new tone. "Heated up" colours are still used by painters today. They have names like **burnt** sienna and **burnt** umber and they can be bought at artist's supplies shops along with the original "earthy" colours such as **raw** sienna, **raw** umber, yellow ochre and red ochre.

Art may well have experimented with colour made from crushed plant leaves, stems and fruit as well (these pigments fade very quickly!).

Mediums ... or media
You need to mix your ground pigments in a medium, otherwise you will find them difficult to apply. They will refuse to stick to your painting surface. Art probably experimented with all sorts of mediums, including:

- water
- a sort of glue made from boiled bits of animals
- his own spit
- his own wee (not recommended!)
- the fatty marrow stuff from the middle of a bone, melted down – (mmmm' tasty!)
- blood

Mix your own pigments with the medium of your choice.

WARNING
DO NOT ABSENT-MINDEDLY LICK YOUR FINGERS WHILST DOING THIS! UUURGH!

Prehistoric paint containers
You will need something to keep your paints in. During prehistoric times there was a world-wide shortage of empty yoghurt cartons so the painters used animal skin pouches, shells and hollowed out bones with a plug at one end. If you cannot find any of these why not use ... err ... yoghurt cartons?

Applying the paint
If you look at pictures of prehistoric paintings you will notice that there are hardly any dribbles or splodges and smudges around them. This tells us that Art and his pals weren't all that keen on finger

28

painting (they probably thought that was for primitives!). They more than likely put the paint on with some of the following items:

- feathers
- a pad made from animal fur
- a bunch of twigs – Art chewed the ends of the twigs to make a crude paint brush
- the hair from animals like badgers, foxes ... or cave people ... which he attached to a stick (the hair **not** the cave people!).

You could try to make your own paintbrush using human hair (your dad's old moustaches, unwanted beards, that kind of thing).

What to paint
Your surface and your paints are ready. Now ... what should you paint? Well, you could:

- invent your own prehistoric scene
- make a copy from a photograph of a cave painting
- paint a picture containing lots of 20th century super-technology, (e.g. computers and lasers) in a prehistoric style, then bury it ... and completely confuse the historians of the future!

Why did the prehistoric artists make the cave paintings?

Lots and lots of theories have been put forward to explain the existence of the cave paintings and some of them are quite convincing, but no one can actually prove that their own particular idea is perfectly correct. Prehistoric people haven't left written explanations for their art (if they had done, they wouldn't be prehistoric would they?). Even if you hopped in your time machine and popped back to ask the cave artists why they did what they did, they probably wouldn't be entirely sure of their reasons for making the pictures, unless it was something like ...

The big bloke with the club said I'd got to do it or he'd bash me!

Various theories that have been put forward to explain the existence of the cave paintings:

1 Prehistoric people were mainly meat-eaters and depended on the animals for food and clothing. There weren't many strict vegetarians about in prehistoric times. We know this because no one has yet discovered a cave full of paintings of Brussels sprouts and cauliflowers and carrots. If you painted the animals it would encourage them to multiply and therefore keep you in bison-burgers, reindeer cutlets and mammoth hair cardigans forever.

2 The hunters felt a kind of affection for the animals

and the pictures were an apology for hunting and killing them. Something like ...

I quite like you and respect you really but, if I don't bump you off, me and my family will starve to death. Therefore, would you mind rubbing your throat up and down on my flint axe-head until you are dead?

3 People thought that animals were somehow sacred and special and painting them was a way of worshipping them.

4 The people who painted the pictures weren't much good at anything else apart from art ... and they had to find *something* to do with their lives.

5 The people had no written language so the paintings were a way of telling stories and leaving records for future generations. The ones containing human figures could be telling the tribe about a heroic deed in cartoon strip form, like in this picture from the caves at Lascaux.

6 The paintings gave the hunters power over the animals and this made both of them less likely to run away at inconvenient moments during the hunt. (It would obviously be extremely inconvenient and would look incredibly silly if both the hunters and the animals ran away at the same time.)

Finishing touches

The reason why the cave paintings were made will always remain a bit of a mystery. You might as well ask:

- why do some people doodle on the neck of the person in front of them during extra-boring maths lessons?
- why do we touch wood for luck when we are about to make a bungee jump from the top of the Post Office Tower using three paper clips and some old knicker elastic?
- why do plumbers whistle tunelessly while they are mending a leek in the vegetable plot?

No one really knows. Not exactly. Humans do lots of odd and bewildering things ... and art is *definitely* one of them.

> **Art-searching – find art for yourself!**
> Art and his contemporaries – Cave paintings located around the Dordogne area of France
> *Animals from the Vogelherd Cave*, Germany (carvings) – Tubingen University, Germany.
> *The Venus of Willendorf*, Austria (small carved female figure) – Natural History Museum, Vienna, Austria.

DOTTY, POTTY, SQUIFFY AND GROTTY

Art the cave painter was a bit of an odd-bod, wasn't he? Then again – if he hadn't been such an independent and imaginative sort of person, he probably wouldn't have bothered making his paintings – and the world would have missed out on some great pictures!

Are you owner of an artistic temperament?

Throughout history, artists have frequently been thought of as being a bit different from other human beings. Creative individuals, like Art, are often said to have something called an "artistic temperament". Perhaps you've got one! Answer the following questionnaire and find out if you are the right sort of person to become an artist. Tick if the answer is "yes" – one tick is worth one creativity point – no cheating!

1 Do *you* ever feel:
a) moody **b)** selfish **c)** impulsive **d)** lacking in self control **e)** really argumentative **f)** persecuted and unloved by the whole world?

2 At any time in your life have you ever had an overwhelming urge to:
a) give away your ears

b) be unkind to a tree

c) behave in an abusive and disrespectful manner towards someone else's socks

d) grow an enormous beard

e) go without washing for longer than you normally do (in other words for *at least* ten weeks)?

3 Are you, or have you ever been:
a) completely addicted to things that aren't good for you **b)** smelly **c)** unwilling to obey rules **d)** inclined to draw attention to yourself by behaving or dressing in a peculiar manner **e)** absent minded?

Scores
If you scored:
15 seek help ... immediately!

Between 12 and 15 Congratulations! You are the proud owner of an artistic temperament. (What do you mean you don't want it – you've got it, and that's that! And no ... you can't be a chartered accountant like your mum! You're *far* too eccentric!)

Between 8 and 12 You're definitely a border-line case. You could have what it takes to be a creative genius. On the other hand, you may well just turn out to be a thoroughly irritating pain in the neck!

Between 1 and 8 Hard luck. You're nowhere nearly temperamental enough ... you're *far* too pleasant and normal sounding.

1 or less Goodness gracious! You're a dull little dishcloth, aren't you? Have you ever considered a career in chartered accountancy?

All kinds of odd characteristics and behaviour seem to go with the job of being an artist. Do artists start out as odd-bods or are they just perfectly normal people who are driven potty by their work at some later stage? After all, art can be very frustrating when things don't go according to plan. It can make you do some very strange things ... as the French Impressionist painter, Claude Monet (1840-1926) found out. Claude was keen on painting directly from Nature – but sometimes – Nature just won't behave itself...

If at first you don't succeed ... turn over a new leaf!

Claude was working on a group of winter land-scapes (no – *not* all at the same time). The pictures were set in very beautiful and spectacular mountainous countryside, and featured an oak tree and a river. Things weren't going at all well...

CLAUDE'S DIARY

Week One: I am being held up by ze awkward Nature (mine actually!) – Oh, if only I wasn't such a fussy pants! Sob. Snivel. Sob. I am not 'appy with my pictures at all! I am going to wipe all ze paint off and start again!

Week two: Mother Nature 'as got ze sulks now – she is raining – my pictures look too gloomy but I must battle on... afterall, I am an ARTIST!

Week three: Quelle horreur! It is snowin'! Now my lovely paintin's are all ze wrong colour!

Week four: Ze snow 'as gone but... ze river is rising – it 'as gone all brown... my lovely river is now ze wrong colour!

Week five: Clouds... sun... then clouds again... then sun... it eez too bright... then it eez too dull... then too bright! It eez drivin' me crackers!

Week Six Sings are gettin' bettur! Ze weather is lovely – but what eez zis? Ze river eez changin' colour... again! And... oh no! It eez dryin' up!

Week Seven: At last everything eez perfect! Today I will do ze big bare oak tree. But WAIT! Where eez it? Some rotten swine 'as pinched it and put zis big leafy one in it's place! Sob, sob, sob... I 'ave just about had my palette full!

Claude had fallen behind with his painting schedule. While he was struggling with the changes in the weather, spring had crept up on him and mischievously covered the oak tree with leaves. The bare tree was to have been the main feature in many of the winter landscapes! So – what do you think Claude did next?

1 He lost his temper, chopped the tree down and made a bonfire from it. Next, he threw his paintings into the flames and danced around, yelling, "Art stinks!" He then returned to Paris and became a professional footballer.

2 He picked all the leaves off the tree whilst muttering "You can't mess with Big Claude and get away with it!"

3 He changed all the paintings from winter to spring scenes.

Answer: 2 (*well … nearly!*).
Claude went to see the local mayor and asked permission to remove the leaves from the tree...

Two men from the local village came with ladders and spent the next two days removing all of the leaves from the tree. Claude was then able to finish his winter landscapes. (And then, did the men stick the leaves back on again?)

Perhaps the life of the Dutch artist, Vincent Van Gogh (1853-1890) was even more frustrating than Claude's. While he was alive most people just didn't seem to recognize his tremendous talent and many of them thought that he was definitely a couple of pigments short of a full palette. His brother, Theo, said that Vincent would eventually be as famous as Beethoven and people would think of him as a genius. As we all now know, Theo's prophecy came true. Vincent is now considered to have been a genius – but he is still equally well remembered for his eccentric behaviour.

And in the blue, red, green and yellow corner ... Vincent Van Gogh!

This is how a 98-year-old man described seeing Vincent when the artist came to paint in the countryside around his home.

> *I used to see him on his knees holding his hands up to his eyes. Then he would sway from side to side, tilting his head from one side to the other. Some people thought he was mad ... I can understand why!*

What a strange way to go about painting a picture! How on earth did Vincent manage to hold his brushes ... and how did he expect to see his subjects if his hands were covering his eyes?

Well – apparently this *wasn't* Vincent's painting

technique – it was just one of his odd little habits. (Perhaps it was his pre-painting warm up exercise ... like a boxer's pre-fight sparring routine? Why not try it in your next art lesson ... or even persuade your teacher to let the whole class have a go. It could be fun!

The old man (who was just a young boy at the time), did actually see Vincent working on a picture. He described how the artist had stripped for action – he was only wearing his underwear and a straw hat ... and was smoking a pipe.

I THOUGHT IT WAS THE MODELS WHO HAD TO TAKE THEIR CLOTHES OFF...

The old man said Vincent would sit staring at the picture for a bit, then leap at it, as if he were going to attack it (the Frank Bruno approach to art!). Then he would paint two or three quick strokes and sit down again (tiring stuff this bare-knuckle painting!). It does sound like rather an unusual technique, doesn't it? But the results were definitely well worth it!

Everyone who knew Vincent says that he lived and worked in the middle of one huge disgusting and chaotic, grotty mess (a bit like the average ten-year-old's bedroom really). He often borrowed his brother's best clothes then left them lying around his studio all jumbled up with his dirty brushes and wet canvases. He even used Theo's clean socks to wipe his brushes on. This led to big rows between the brothers (especially if Theo happened to be wearing the socks at the time!).

Vincent was a very intense and emotional type of person who had problems keeping his friends. One day he was feeling particularly unhappy because his painter pal, Paul Gauguin, had just given him the brush-off. Vincent was so upset about falling out with Paul that he cut off a piece of his ear (his own – not Paul's!). He then gave it to a girlfriend, saying ...

At times in his life, Vincent was a very lonely and troubled person. When he wasn't painting, he wrote lots and lots of letters to his brother, Theo, whom he relied upon for encouragement and support. The letters didn't say things like "Brushes dirty again – send fresh socks!" They were full of Vincent's most personal thoughts about his art. Anyone reading them can see that his painting meant everything to him – which really makes it extra sad that he never had much success in selling his wonderful pictures while he was alive.

Stan, the baggage man

Sir Stanley Spencer (1891-1959) was a British artist who painted lots of scenes from the Bible which he brought up to date by setting them in his home village of Cookham and portraying the ordinary people of his own time as the main characters. Like Vincent, some people thought Sir Stan was a bit eccentric. This could have been because:

1 He liked to use toilet rolls as sketch pads – they were so convenient!

2 He was fond of pushing a pram around. You probably don't think this is particularly remarkable – lots of dads take their children out for a walk, don't they? Well ... the pram didn't contain Stanley's bouncing baby – it contained his bouncing brushes and colours and easel and canvases, which he was transporting to his favourite painting spots! Stan found the pram's folding hood particularly useful for protecting his precious paintings from sudden showers of rain.

3 He wasn't too keen on washing – for most of his life, Stanley only had a cold water supply in his house. Perhaps this was why he often looked like he hadn't washed for a long time and was always a bit down-at-heel.

Sometimes when he turned up at places like posh restaurants and galleries the doormen would refuse to let him in because he was so small and scruffy.

> *You can't come in here, you horrible little man. You're far too small and messy. Go away and grow bigger ... and have a bath while you're at it!*

When Stan's pictures began to sell for large amounts of money he was tracked down by a Rolls Royce salesman who hoped to sell the newly famous and wealthy artist a super smart motor-car. When the salesman actually met Stanley he soon realized that he wasn't the type of person to be bothered about shiny status symbols and quickly left him alone.

Stanley trained to be a painter at a famous art school called the Slade. He was such a brilliant artist that he won an award and was summoned to a special prize-giving ceremony in London. As Stan was getting out of his railway carriage at Euston Station, a posh-looking gentleman mistook the scruffy young artist for a station porter and whistled him, saying, "Carry my bags!" Being an obliging and helpful kind of young chap, Stanley did as he was told and obediently carried the gentleman's bags across London (it's just what you'd have done in the same circumstances, isn't it?). The gentleman then gave Stanley a tip and they went their separate ways.

A bit later on Stanley attended the presentation ceremony. When he went up to receive his award he was astonished to discover that the special guest handing out the prizes ... was the same person whose bags he'd carried from the station earlier that day! No doubt the man handing out the awards was even more baffled and amazed than Stan was!

"I'll go to any lengths to get it right!"

Although artists like Claude, Vincent and Stanley had a rather unconventional approach to their life and work, they didn't really seem to care what other people thought about them. After all, art must come first – and it's the results that count ... isn't it?

The 18th-century portrait painter, Thomas Gainsborough, was prepared to go to tremendous lengths to achieve the right effect in his pictures – he painted with brushes that were *six feet* long! Why did he use the mega-brushes?

1 Thomas was an ex-snooker professional and the really long brush handles made him feel extra confident.

2 The smell of oil paints brought him out in a rash and this was the only way he could keep well away from his whiffy materials.

3 He liked to stand at the same distance from his canvases as he was standing from his model.

4 He was very long sighted and couldn't afford spectacles.

Answer: 3 Thomas earned his living from painting the portraits of rich and famous people and this was a technique he used to ensure absolute accuracy in perspective and proportion.

When he wasn't doing portraits, Thomas painted marvellous landscapes. His methods for these were equally unusual. Rather than go out to Nature, he frequently brought Nature into his studio – sometimes bringing whole tree branches indoors to sketch from. He even had a donkey tethered just a few feet away from his easel so that he could make accurate drawings of it (and have someone intelligent to chat to?).

Thomas would have probably brought whole fields and forests into his workroom if he could have done, but as this was impossible he made his own miniature landscapes to copy from. He used:

PIECES OF GLASS TO REPRESENT STREAMS AND PONDS

BROCCOLI FOR TREES THAT WERE IN LEAF

TWIGS FOR BARE TRUNKS & BRANCHES

STONES AND LUMPS OF COAL FOR LARGE ROCKS AND BOULDERS

SAND OR CLAY FOR THE GROUND

BITS OF MOSS FOR BUSHES

He then added little farm animals that he'd modelled from clay. Finally he lit a candle or an oil lamp near his composition so that he could create the effect of sunlight and shadow on the scene.

Thomas's method sounds like fun doesn't it – why not create your own miniature Gainsborough style landscape to draw from, but use a torch or electric lamp instead of a candle – it's much safer!

It's quite difficult to discover what some artists were really like because they often lived a lonely life and never had too many friends. Aaah! Then again, if you go around saying things like, "A thousand artists should be killed every year!" you shouldn't be at all surprised if people start avoiding you. That's what Paul Cézanne (1839-1906) once said. He also said, "I want to stun all of Paris with an apple!" And that's what he did. He painted stunning pictures of apples (plus a few other things). Now there's an idea! If we can't ask Paul's pals what kind of a chap he was – why not talk to one of his models?

45

Living with a genius – an artist's model remembers
by Ann Apple (*1877-1877*)

I don't like to brag or anything, but … you know that Paul Cézanne, the famous painter, well, I was his favourite model. In fact, I think I can definitely say … I was the apple of his eye! You probably know me actually, I'm the third apple from the left in his Still Life with Oranges and Apples. That's me in the Jeu De Paume Museum in Paris.

Yes, it was me who was the original inspiration behind all those still-life fruit pictures that are so famous nowadays. I still remember the very first words Cézanne said to me as he picked me out from the rest of the bunch.

"Oh … what a dear little sphere!" is what he said. "All of nature's wondrous mystery and beauty is embodied in your cute little curves. You look almost good enough to eat … Ha, ha … only joking … my little pippin!" And then he patted my bottom most affectionately … talk about blush!

The whole thing began one really hot day in the summer of 1895. A whole bunch of us apples were hanging around in Provence, in the south of France. There we were, dangling from our branches, minding our own business and complementing each other on how nice and fat and pink we were turning in that lovely summer sun when, all of a sudden, we saw this red-haired chap crawling under the bit of broken fence in the corner of our orchard. He was muttering to himself and looking around in a really shifty way. I can tell you ... he gave us all a bit of a fright, what with that fierce pointy beard and those menacing eyebrows of his.

"Oh dear, he looks rather threatening, doesn't he?" whimpered an extremely nervous Golden Delicious, "I hope he doesn't pick on my bough!"

"Don't worry! It's Paul Cézanne," whispered a pear on a neighbouring tree, "he's an Impressionist."

"Oh, that sounds like fun," squeaked a rather silly young apple. "Who does he impersonate? Napoleon ... or Queen Victoria ... or just well known music-hall acts?"

"Not that kind of an impressionist, you fool!" snapped the pear.

IMPRESSIONIST   POST-IMPRESSIONIST

"He's a painter; some people say he's a post-impressionist, actually – he's very respectable and everything ... the only thing is, he's got this thing about scrumping. He's obsessed with fruit. He can't leave us alone!"

The pear was right. I suddenly felt myself being twisted off my twig and dropped into the pocket of Cézanne's velvet jacket with some of my chums and, the next thing we knew, we were all in his studio.

He began arranging us on the table in front of his

easel straightaway. He couldn't seem to get us placed to his satisfaction though. No sooner had he got us in one arrangement, than he'd be moving us around again.

"It's got to look absolutely natural ... absolument naturelle!" he kept saying to himself and then, he began singing! (To the tune of the hokey-cokey, would you believe?)

You put your fruit bowl there, your apples here,
                    your milk jug there
              Then you move them all about.
      Oh, oh, the spheres, the cones and cylinders!
      Oh, oh, the spheres, the cones and cylinders!
                 That's what it's all about!

Well, at the time, I hadn't the faintest idea what it was all about! But now – I understand every word of it! Well you would, wouldn't you, if you'd spent about a hundred years with every art nut in the world standing in front of your portrait and calling you a masterpiece and going on about how brilliantly Cézanne showed the solid shapes of things? I still remember the day Picasso and his mate, Georges Braque, came in – not long after Cézanne's death.

"You know, that Cézanne was a really ace dude!" said Picasso, as he admired us apples. "He's kind of inspired us crazy cats of this new century to do our own thing and paint any way we feel like painting. It was really far out and modern the way he expressed everything's shape in terms of cones and spheres and cylinders..."

"...and cubes!" added George.

"Yes ... and them," said Picasso.

"That's what we're always doing, Pablo!" said

48

George, "painting everything so it looks like a load of cubes and that."

"Hey, it is … isn't it?" said Picasso. "That gives me an idea! Why don't we call ourselves the Cubists?"

"All right, then!" cried George, "though I'm not sure whether it'll catch on." As you probably know, "the Cubists" is exactly what they did become known as! As for us apples, that's another story. Cézanne was an extremely slow painter. After about three weeks we started to lose our looks. Our complexions went all wrinkly and our lovely tans faded … and he'd still only sketched in our general shapes!

We began to sense that somehow, he didn't feel quite the same about us. And we were right! Guess what the rotter did? He only went and replaced us with some younger and prettier fruit! But that's not the worst of it! Just to add insult to injury, him and that Pierre Renoir turned us old models into a fruit crumble and had us for Sunday lunch. Well, that's artists for you! Dead fickle! It's definitely me in the painting though, third from the left…

me!

Cézanne painted apples (and lots of other things) like no one had ever painted them before. Other painters had made great efforts to make their apples as much like an apple and as less like a painting as they possibly could. They'd used all sorts of skills and techniques to do this – like going out of their way to make their brush strokes so invisible that you'd swear the apple had just grown right there in the picture rather than having been artificially created with bristles and pigment.

Cézanne didn't care if you could see his brush strokes. He wanted them to be seen – and they actually look really interesting. You know, his apple is a "painting" of an apple rather than an "almost real" pretend apple. He was far more interested in showing the way the shapes and colours of things related to each other. Cézanne wanted the objects in his pictures to fit together as harmoniously as possible – which is one of the reasons he took so much time and trouble arranging his still-lifes.

Many critics of his day thought his work was worthless. One said it was, "the greatest joke in art for 15 years!" and another said, "If we agree with Mr Cézanne we might as well set fire to the Louvre!" (The Louvre is the national museum and art gallery of France.) Cézanne didn't let them put him off though. He carried on working away in the unique style that was to have such a big influence on many artists who came after him.

Despite what the critics said about him, Cézanne definitely didn't want to burn down the Louvre – but another artist thought it was quite a good idea.

War is good! – burn the museums! Tamara de Lempicka and the fanatical Futurists

Some hot-headed artists become so obsessed with their BIG new idea that they just have to carry it out immediately. The Polish artist, Tamara de Lempicka (1898-1980), was just such an impulsive woman of action – she didn't let anything stand in her way. Once she made her mind up to do something ... she did it! Like the time she and her friends burned down the world-famous Louvre art museum ... well ... almost!

Tamara's friends were a group of artists and poets called the Futurists who got together at the beginning of the 20th century. They were all really excited about the modern, new-fangled, exciting, machiney things that were starting to appear in those days – like wooden flying machines – and motor cars that could go as fast as ... 30 miles an hour! (Yes, 30 miles an hour – a real beige knuckle experience!). Their hero and leader was a poet called Marinetti. He once said that a racing car was a far more beautiful thing than a mouldy old masterpiece painting. (Yes, but did he ever try hanging a Ferrari on his living room wall – it doesn't half make a mess of the picture hooks!)

Marinetti said that all the old art should be completely destroyed in as violent a manner as possible. He even said that war was a good thing! One day Tamara and the Futurists were sitting in a café in Paris listening to Marinetti who was standing on a table and making a speech about getting rid of all the old art in the world.

But wait! The Louvre was … more than two horse-drawn tram rides away … they couldn't rampage that far – they'd be worn out! What were they to do? The situation was becoming tense and dangerous. The crowd had swollen (it was a good café) and they had now turned into an angry mob. The cries of "BURN THE LOUVRE!" became even more heated. Direct action was needed.

As Tamara gazed adoringly into the eyes of her hero, she suddenly realized that she alone had it in her power to change the whole course of history. For there, sitting outside the café, was her very own symbol of speed and power and thrusting technology. Yes, that was it! They would use her very own little motor car to go and destroy all of the old art!

"Maestro!" she cried to Marinetti (it wasn't a Maestro actually – it was a Renault – but that's not the point is it?), "my little car is outside ... we can use it if you want to go and burn the Louvre!"

It was a perfect idea, and so fitting! It didn't even matter that it was only a very small car. Tamara could nip backwards and forwards between the café and the Louvre and ferry the rampaging mob there in shifts ... two or three at a time (perhaps the smaller Futurists could sit on the knees of the bigger ones?). She could even ask them for petrol money! Brilliant! The decision was made and the Futurists all charged out of the café. At that moment ... disaster struck!

 But why?

1 Tamara suddenly remembered that one of her paintings was hanging in the Louvre and she decided she didn't want to be a Futurist any more.
2 They got lost on their way to the gallery.

3 Tamara's car had been towed away for being illegally parked.

4 They remembered it was Sunday ... and the Louvre was closed all day.

Answer: 3.

Tamara's little car wasn't there! There was just a car-sized parking space at the side of the pavement where the machine of the future had stood not ten minutes earlier. Those rotten unsporting French traffic police were just being too futuristic now! They had towed the car away. Silly Tamara hadn't noticed she had left it in restricted waiting area! So, the Louvre didn't get burned down after all. Perhaps they would go and burn it another time. They could even make a day of it and bring sandwiches and have a picnic in the Jardin des Tuileries.

Before the Futurists got the chance to have another crack at burning the Louvre, their ideas began to lose popularity. The First World War was still fresh in the memories of many people and they were very much aware that millions of young men had been killed by the very new-fangled technology that Marinetti and his followers had thought so much of – like extra-efficient machine guns and tanks and aeroplanes. Their fanatical obsessions suddenly began to look a bit ridiculous and quite soon, many artists forgot all about Futurism. The Louvre Museum's still there though ... and it's full of brilliant art – all thanks to those wonderful French traffic wardens.

The sorry story of Maurice Utrillo – tearaway, painter and sozzlepot

Some artists have had a reputation for being far too fond of things that are bad for them, like too much alcohol. Drink often has a devastating effect on the progress of great geniuses, especially if they spill it all over their work. Maurice Utrillo (1888-1955) was actually recommended to take up art as a way of curing his addiction to strong drink. The results were amazing!

5 BY THE TIME YOU WERE 13 YOU WERE CONSTANTLY BUNKING OFF SCHOOL AND MEETING UP WITH BAD CHARACTERS. IT WAS THEM WHO TAUGHT YOU HOW TO GET SQUIFFY!

SORRY GRAN.

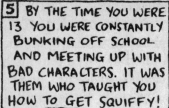

6 BY THE TIME YOU WERE IN YOUR LATE TEENS YOU WERE A TOTAL SOZZLEPOT... **AND** YOU WERE BEHAVING VERY BADLY! DO YOU REMEMBER THE TIME YOU LOST YOUR JOB AT THE BANK?

I CERTAINLY REMEMBER IT!

!?

7 IT'S MY BOSS, OLD WOTZISNAME!

YES IT IS, MAURICE... AND I'VE STILL GOT THE LUMP ON MY HEAD WHERE YOU BROKE YOUR UMBRELLA OVER IT...

SORRY WOTZISNAME!

8 I WAS VERY UPSET ABOUT ALL THIS. I THOUGHT "WHAT OUR MAURICE NEEDS IS A NICE HOBBY - SOMETHING TO KEEP HIS MIND OFF THE DRINK..." THAT'S WHEN I HAD MY GREAT IDEA. HE COULD TAKE UP **PAINTING!** I GAVE HIM SOME PAINTS AND BRUSHES AND HE TOOK TO IT LIKE A DUCK TO WATER-COLOURS!

9 IT WAS OIL-COLOURS ACTUALLY, MUM...

THAT'S NOT THE POINT.

SORRY MUM

10 ONCE HE GOT GOING THERE WAS NO STOPPING HIM! HE WAS ESPECIALLY BRILLIANT AT PARIS STREET SCENES... IN JUST **4 YEARS** HE PAINTED...

OVER **TWELVE HUNDRED** PICTURES - INCLUDING 200 THAT ARE NOW THOUGHT TO BE MASTERPIECES!

WOW!

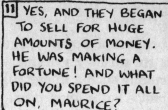

Bacon ... with oysters ... boot polish ... and lots of Vim

Francis Bacon was also rather fond of alcohol ... and gambling ... and shellfish. He wasn't an ordinary kind of person – is there actually such a thing? His art is extraordinarily brilliant – but a lot of people find it very disturbing.

His pictures are often of people who look as if they're in great pain, or have let their figures go rather badly. This is because Francis changed the expressions and body positions of his subjects in a really dramatic way. His life style was as original and as unconventional as his painting style.

1 Francis was addicted to oysters and gambling. He actually stole someone else's money in order to gamble, then later returned it when he had a big win at the casino.

2 He was very fond of black hair. Unfortunately, his own hair was light brown, so he regularly coloured it with black boot polish. One day when he was gambling in a very hot casino his boot-polish hair dye melted then dribbled down his forehead.

3 To give himself that all-round ring of confidence and a whiter than white smile, he cleaned his teeth with Vim! (old-fashioned toilet cleaner).

How Francis gave the Pope the screaming ab daubs

When he was a boy, Francis bought a book called *Diseases of the Mouth*. This was to have a lasting influence on his later art work.

While the other children were out playing tag, Francis wiled away many a happy afternoon gazing wistfully at his beloved *Diseases of the Mouth* book. The enchanting illustrations of all the totally appalling things you can get wrong with your mouth were to be a great inspiration to him in later life.

When he grew up he painted a series of pictures that were influenced by his admiration for a painting of Pope Innocent X by the Spanish painter, Velasquez (1599-1660) ... and his life-long interest in medical books. Many of these pictures are of popes with horribly disfigured mouths who seem to be having the screaming ab dabs.

Francis said he wanted their screams to look "like a sunset by Monet". You could say the Screaming Popes all look a bit "down in the mouth". This may be because Francis has painted them trapped inside glass cases – or perhaps it's just because they've got rather painful cold sores?

Sometimes the people in Francis's pictures are so disfigured that it's hard to recognize who they are. This once led to a very awkward situation...

Sainsbury's Bacon causes journalist great embarrassment

The Sainsbury family (the ones that own a chain of British supermarkets) have always been collectors of paintings, including works by Francis. Francis actually painted several portraits of members of the Sainsbury family in his own unique and unforgettable style. One day a journalist was admiring one of these pictures.

Oower! How embarrassing! No doubt the journalist would have wished that the ground (or one of Francis's screaming popes) could have swallowed him on the spot.

Confessions of Joseph Mallord William Turner (1775-1851)

Many great artists have been thought of as a bit odd by the rest of society. The English landscape painter, Turner, is now considered to have been a genius, but if you'd known him when he was alive you might have had good reason for thinking he was slightly batty. In his own words ...

I put in bids for my own pictures at auctions. Why? In order to bump up the price, of course ... I had to eat you know!

If anyone tried to watch me when I was painting, I immediately covered up my work so that people wouldn't copy my great techniques.

I got so fed up with the critics saying that my paintings were rubbish that I changed my name to Admiral Puggy Booth – just so that I could get a bit of peace and quiet to do my work.

I once had myself lashed to a mast of a ship during a really fierce storm at sea, so that I could carry on sketching the terrible weather conditions without being swept overboard. I was there for four hours but it was well worth it!

When the Houses of Parliament caught fire, I hired a boat and had myself rowed across the River Thames so that I could get as close to the blaze as possible. I then painted on-the-spot watercolour pictures of the whole scene.

I was once in a stage coach that was crossing the Alps. The coach overturned at the top of a high and dangerous pass on Mount Cenis. A scene of chaos followed. The weather was atrocious, the coach doors were frozen shut, the guide and the driver argued about whose fault the crash was and began to fight. It was a wonderful scene, too good to miss. I immediately got out my materials and began sketching the whole thing!

Finishing touches

If Turner hadn't been such an individualist he may never have picked up a paint brush – and then he wouldn't have left the British nation (and the rest of the world) more than 19,000 fantastic drawings and paintings to enjoy, would he? Like many artists, he had strong ideas about what he wished to achieve and the way he would set about it. Being a free spirit – sticking to your ideas, come what may – and not following the crowd, is perhaps an essential part of being an artist, even if it means that you are thought of as odd or different (or completely crackers!) by the rest of society.

Art-searching – find art for yourself!
Claude Monet – *Flood Waters* – 1896 – National Gallery, London
Vincent Van Gogh – *Wheatfield With Cypresses* – 1889 – National Gallery
Stanley Spencer – *Resurrection, Cookham* – 1923-26 – Tate Gallery, London
Thomas Gainsborough – *Wooded Landscape With Cattle By A Pool* – 1782 – Gainsborough's House, Sudbury, Suffolk.
Paul Cézanne – *Still Life With Apples and Melons* – 1890-94 – National Gallery
Maurice Utrillo – *Rue De Mont Cenis à Montmartre* – 1916 – Pompidou Centre, Paris
Tamara De Lempicka – *Blue Abstract* – 1955 – Musée National d'Art Moderne, Paris
Francis Bacon – *Head Surrounded By Sides of Beef* – 1954 – Art Institute of Chicago, U.S.A.
Joseph Turner – *The Burning Of The Houses Of Parliament* – 1834 – Clore Gallery, London

THE ARTISTS WHO TRIED TO REACH THE PARTS OF OUR BRAINS THAT OTHER ART DOESN'T REACH

One group of artists convinced almost everyone that they were crazy. They were called the Surrealists and they deliberately created art that was extremely weird ... and slightly spooky! One of the leading Surrealists was the Spanish artist, Salvador Dali (1904-1979). At the first International Exhibition of Surrealist Art in 1938 he said people would experience:

- twelve hundred bags of coal
- smells from Brazil
- a monster pair of underpants as big as a whole room!

- The exhibition was in complete darkness and the visitors were given lamps in order to see the exhibits.
- They saw a woman with a parrot's head. She had little spoons stuck all over her. (What a stirring sight!)

- They saw another woman in a taxi full of plants – live snails were crawling all over her face. Every now and again it started raining ... inside the taxi!
- Another exhibit was a cup and a saucer – completely covered in animal fur. (Someone obviously wasn't using the right sort of washing-up liquid!)

It was all very strange. That's because the Surrealists tried to use their subconscious minds to make their art. Does this mean that they:

1 battered each other completely senseless before they began work?

2 painted while they were asleep?

3 painted with brushes fastened to the backs of their heads?

4 were really interested in the world of dreams and the weird and bizarre thoughts that float around the darkest corners of our minds?

Answer: 4.

The weird world of our subconscious minds

About a hundred years ago a man called Sigmund Freud started to poke and pry into the hidden bits of people's brains – no, not with his fingers – with questions! He talked to people while they were hypnotized, or feeling really relaxed. He made an amazing discovery! He discovered that we've all got loads of thoughts and feelings and memories ... that we don't even know we've got!

Sigmund Freud believed that these thoughts were hidden in a kind of secret cupboard in our heads. He called this cupboard our subconscious, or our unconscious mind. He said that when we have a dream it is a bit like getting a peep into the cupboard of our subconscious.

When the Surrealists found out about this, they said, "Wow! This sounds like fun! Let's open *our* subconscious cupboards and make art about the things we discover. We can do paintings of dreams and have events and exhibitions where we act out our weirdest ideas and feelings!"

Two Surrealists have a Surrealist chat

Surrealist arty-facts

1 Surrealism means 'beyond the real.'

2 Many of the Surrealist artists tried to live their everyday lives in a Surreal way.

3 Some of their paintings are painted so realistically that they almost look like photographs. When you look at them it feels as if they had smuggled a camera into their "land of nod" and taken snapshots of their dreams.

4 Some surrealists produced their artwork while they were in a kind of hypnotic trance (just like many children produce their schoolwork).

5 Many modern day T.V. and newspaper advertisers use strange Surrealist-style ads in order to catch people's attention. For example, the one for cider where the dog walks across the pub ceiling.

The Surrealist exhibition that caused a bit of a kerfuffle

A lot of people thought the Surrealists were barmy. At one exhibition of their art they also showed a

Surrealist film called *Un Chien Andalou (An Andalusian Dog)*. Important note to all squeamish readers – please do not read the next sentence! In one scene in the film someone's eyeball is sliced with a razor blade. OK you can carry on reading now.

A group of visitors didn't like the exhibition, or the film, one little bit. What happened next? Did the visitors:

1 raise their eyebrows and make "Tut, tut!" noises?
2 throw purple ink at the cinema screen?
3 let off stink bombs and smoke bombs?
4 slash and smash the Surrealists' paintings to pieces?
5 bash other people with clubs?

Answer:
They did all of these things ... and then they felt lots better.

Create your own Surrealist dreamscape ... or nightmare scenario!

You can create Surrealist-type dream picture ... even if you are not a mad genius!

What you'll need

- some cheese
- paints and paper
- glue
- scissors
- plenty of unwanted magazines and newspapers

With these simple items you too can conjure up a startling dream or nightmare scene that is so bizarre and out of this world that it will scare the bow-ties off passing art historians.

All you have to do
- Eat the cheese (optional), go to bed, sleep, have lots of strange dreams.

- Wake up (optional) – remember your dreams (write them down before they disappear!).

- Make a composition from your notes and memories using a painting background and photographs cut from the magazines.

- Keep rearranging the images until a really weird picture emerges. Let your imagination, your dream memories and perhaps even your subconscious control your thoughts and actions.

Picture idea
This is for people who are always asleep during their dreams and therefore can never remember them.

- Attach the heads of humans to the bodies of animals (or the other way round).
- Then set them in your own painted landscape where the sky is full of out of place objects, like rowing boats, or jars of jam.

Dali-data

Salvador Dali was full of bright ideas. Here are a few of them.

WARNING
DO NOT TRY THIS AT HOME —
OR ANYWHERE ELSE!

Salvador Dali's wacky wheezes: number one – the exploding duck

One day Salvador decided he would like to have his photograph taken ... with a duck. He went to his photographer friend and said, "Here's what we'll do. We'll take a duck and put some dynamite in its bottom. When the duck explodes I will jump and you take the photograph!"

His friend was a little bit surprised and said, "We will be put in prison if we start exploding ducks!"

Salvador thought for a moment, then said, "You're

70

right. Let's take some cats and splash them with water instead." Which is exactly what they did.

Wacky wheeze number two: the art lecture

Salvador was going to give a lecture and slide show on Surrealist art. He thought he ought to dress up for the occasion. What do you think he chose to wear?

1 his jeans and T-shirt
2 his suit
3 his pyjamas

Obvious really, isn't it? He decided to go for the suit of course ... the deep-sea diving one with the radiator cap from a Mercedes car attached to the helmet and the little plastic hands stuck to the middle section. And to make sure he looked totally groovy he added some really subtle finishing touches to the outfit, like a jewelled dagger tucked in the belt ... *and* a billiard cue ... and two enormous Irish wolfhounds (the wolfhounds weren't tucked in the belt – he wasn't *that* surreal – he had them on a lead!).

"Am I dreaming? This is quite *un*-real!" thought several members of his audience as he walked on to the lecture platform ... then again ... that was the whole idea, wasn't it?

The lecture is breath-taking!

During the slide show Salvador discovered that the diving suit was perhaps not a wise choice of evening wear after all. People couldn't actually hear what he was saying. Even worse, the helmet cut off his air supply and he began to suffocate! He signalled frantically for someone to help him but his spellbound audience didn't seem to realize that their guest lecturer was dying before their very eyes.

Eventually the lecture organizers spotted that something was the matter and made a desperate attempt to rescue Salvador from his killer clobber. They couldn't unfasten the nuts and bolts that held the helmet in place so Salvador just carried on dying! Someone rushed off and found a workman who was kind enough to loan them his spanner. Salvador was rescued from the diving suit just in the nick of time!

Wacky wheeze number three: the dream ball

Salvador organized a kind of Surrealist disco. The guests were greeted by a doorman wearing roses and sitting in a rocking chair on the pavement. They then had to get past a huge block of ice tied up in red ribbon that was partly blocking the doorway. Once they were inside they danced to music coming from a dead cow wearing a wedding veil. Its stomach had been removed and replaced by a record player – (just like your average end of term disco really!).

Salvador Dali's useful inventions

At first people were afraid to buy Salvador's paintings because they were so weird (the paintings, not the people). As a way of making money he decided to invent things that would be useful. They included:

1 a settee that looked exactly like the lips of the famous film star Mae West.

2 false fingernails with little mirrors built into them so that the wearer could admire themselves whenever they felt a bit vain.

3 Furniture made from bakelite (an early type of plastic) that was moulded to the shape of its owner's body.

4 Shoes with springs in them, to make walking more fun.

Does this last idea make you think of modern sports trainers with their built in air-cushions? Many of Salvador's inventions were considered shocking and outrageous in his day, but 50 years on, they don't seem quite so bizarre. In fact some of them seem quite useful. They actually use one of those lip-shaped settees on one of the late-night TV shows. Like Vincent Van Gogh and many other artists, Salvador is now thought to have been ahead of his time in many ways.

René Magritte and the pipe which was not a pipe

LE BRUSSELS SPOUT 17th Septembre

NOT A PIPE? VOUS MUST BE JOKING!

Those barmy Surrealists are at it again. Come off it, René, who do you think you're kidding? So-called Surrealist artist, René Magritte, has painted this picture of a pipe. Guess what the potty painter has done! He's only gone and called the painting *This is Not a Pipe*! Come off it, Monsieur Magritte! Who *do* you think you're kidding? Us *Spout* readers aren't stupid you know! Of

Ceci n'est pas une pipe

course it's a pipe! What else could it be? Next thing we know, you'll be trying to tell us it's a hollow, curved, wooden device for inhaling the fumes of smouldering dried vegetable matter? Ha ha ha! Pull the other one!

And if that's not enough he's done this other one. In this

74

one it's raining not raindrops but men, dozens of them! We ask you … does he expect us to believe this would really happen?

We showed a copy of the picture to Monsieur Michel Poisson (Fish), a regular *Spout* reader and amateur weather forecaster.

"It's like a very weird dream, unreal and completely unbelievable!" said Monsieur Poisson, "I mean, I've never come across a weather forecast that says, 'The morning will be clear and dry followed by light showers of identical bowler-hatted men wearing black overcoats,' have you? Ha ha ha!"

The *Spout* says, "The joke's on you, René! You Surrealists really are a shower, aren't you? Wise up and get … real!

The *Daily Spout* journalists obviously didn't realize that René's picture of men descending from the sky was a dream painting. Nor did they get his point about the picture of the pipe. He was trying to say that the picture was *definitely not* a pipe. And he was right. It wasn't a pipe … it was a piece of canvas covered in paint marks that were arranged in such a way that they gave the impression or illusion of a pipe! What you see is what you believe!

Max Ernst and the flabbergasting floorboards

Max Ernst (1891-1976) was a German Surrealist artist who enjoyed the occasional bit of meditation and hallucination. One day he was sitting in a seaside pub having a quiet think and a packet of dry roasted peanuts. All of a sudden he noticed the floorboards. He instantly became mesmerized by their fascinating rough surface! He just couldn't stop staring at it! Unable to contain himself any longer he covered them with sheets of paper and began to rub them with a pencil. The rest of the customers were bewildered, but Max was deliriously happy. He had discovered the art technique now known as frottage! Frottage is French for rubbing. You may well be wondering why we don't just call it rubbing? Well, it doesn't sound so exciting or clever, does it?

Max also developed lots of other enjoyable art techniques with which to while away the long winter's evenings. They include oscillation, grattage, collage and decalcomania. You can enjoy all of these in the privacy of your own home, and you don't even have to be a Surrealist.

ACTIVITY

Create your own masterpiece using the techniques of Max Ernst

Number one: oscillation

- Tie a piece of string to a paint pot or yoghurt pot with a very small hole in the bottom then dangle it over a large piece of paper.
- Now make swinging movements with it – *not* with the paper! With the *pot*!
- You should now see interesting patterns forming on the canvas (or up your bedroom wall).
- Nothing's happened? Well ... try putting some paint in the pot!

Number two: decalcomania

- Cover a piece of paper with paint then press a second unpainted piece of paper on top of it. Peel it back.

- Press the second piece of paper on to a third unpainted piece of paper. Press the third piece of paper on to a fourth piece and so on and so forth. Each piece of paper will have a different paint texture on it as the amount of paint gets less and less.

You can actually carry on this activity for as long as you wish, but beware of becoming a raving decalco-maniac. These people have been known to get so carried away with this activity that they have used up a whole rain forest in one afternoon!

Number three: frottage and grattage
With these activities you have to let your unconscious mind get in touch with an interesting textured surface – just like Max did when he was in the pub. It isn't even absolutely necessary to go to a pub to do them.
- Any old surface will do as long as it's not too smooth.

HMMM
HELLO GRAN

- Use something like a piece of rough wood or sacking, or an obliging rhinoceros.

IT WASN'T ME! IT WAS MY UNCONSCIOUS MIND!

- Put your paper on the surface and rub away with your pencil. You will probably sense your subconscious mind getting in touch with the object you are frottaging.

Grattage is similar to frottage but instead of using pencil you use paint.

- You place your paper on the textured surface and put a small amount of paint on it.

- You then scrape the paint across the paper using something like a piece of wood or a very dry paint brush. The pattern made by the paint should resemble the texture of your chosen surface.

All of the varied patterns and textures you have made in these activities are intended to get your imagination going. You may see interesting shapes in your results which you can go on to develop into recognizable forms.

79

When you have finished these activities you can assemble all of the pieces into a collage by cutting and pasting them to another sheet of paper or a backing board.

Max combined all of these techniques in his very beautiful work of art called *Vox Angelica* (*Angelic Voice*).

Finishing touches

Many artists express their subconscious thoughts through their work. Sometimes they don't even know they're doing it

Question: Does Darren have a subconscious desire to see terrible things happen to his poor teacher?

Answer: No, of course not! Darren's teacher is Mr Smith. Darren has a subconscious desire to see terrible things happen to his dentist.

Art-searching – find art for yourself!
René Magritte – *This Is Not a Pipe* – 1928-29 –
William N. Copley Collection, New York, U.S.A.
Salvador Dali – *Soft Construction With Boiled
Beans*, "Premonition Of Civil War" – 1936 –
Philadelphia Museum of Art, U.S.A.
Max Ernst – *They Have Stayed Too Long In The
Forest* – Saarland Museum, Saarbrucken,
Germany

ARTISTS WANTED
~APPLY WITHIN~
Earn a fortune! Your Doodles Could Make You Oodles (Then again... your scribbles might not even pay for nibbles!)

Suffering for their art – a series of sob stories

Salvador Dali eventually made so much money from his art that he was able to build himself a luxurious castle to live in. Not all artists are this fortunate – sometimes the world fails to recognize their creative genius and they spend the whole of their lives in poverty. Which would you rather be ... a penniless painter or a millionaire art megastar? If you are thinking of becoming an artist there are a number of career paths open to you. Chose the route you think would best suit you. Would you like to be:

1 really poor for a while ... then fabulously rich?

2 really poor ... then fabulously rich ... then fabulously poor?

3 fabulously rich ... then fabulously richer?

4 really poor for years and years then fabulously rich ... but dead?

5 really poor ... followed by so broke you're forced to sell your teeth?

Unfortunately, most artists don't usually get to choose their career route – *it* usually chooses *them*. Some are smiled on by good fortune while others are tormented by fickle fate (or tickled feet). So, who are the jammy bodgers, who are the millionaire maestros and who are the doomed daubers? Read on and find out...

Pablo Picasso's remarkable rise to riches

At the beginning of his career, the Spanish artist, Pablo Picasso (1881-1973), lived in terrible poverty in Paris. He was so poor that he couldn't even afford enough to eat. It's said that he used to steal milk from doorsteps. He was even forced to share a bed with a poet, but not at the same time. They went to bed in shifts – Pablo kipped in the day and painted at night while his poet pal, Max Jacob, slept at night and worked by day. Pablo and Max also shared an overcoat and a top hat (which must have been very uncomfortable ... and embarrassing!).

One day, when they were feeling particularly fed up with being poor and hungry, the two young artists went mad and bought a sausage. Unfortunately it was a very cheap sausage and instead of

83

being full of succulent meat it was full of succulent gas and when they tried to cook it, it exploded (well it would, wouldn't it – it was a banger!). Pablo remembered this exploding sausage for the rest of his life and Max even wrote poems about it.

Despite all of his problems Pablo continued to work his socks off at being an artist – he was determined to be a success. He couldn't afford to pay artists' models so he painted the people of his local area – who were also poor. His pictures from around this time (1901-1904) are full of poor people all looking cold and thin and miserable and hungry, just like he was.

As well as being poor, the people in Picasso's paintings were also blue – in fact whole pictures were blue. This was because he used lots of different shades of blue paint to give his work a mood of bleakness and despair and loneliness. Picasso himself may well have been blue – the Paris winters were freezing. As a result of all this blueness, this period in Picasso's life is now referred to as his "Blue Period". (What a brilliant idea.) It was soon followed by:

- His "Pink Period" (where he cheered up a bit and painted pictures with a rosy glow).
- His "Negro Period" (where he got even more cheerful and was influenced by the colours and shapes of African art).
- His "Cubist Period" (where he felt obsolutely great and was influenced by Cézanne).

As his various periods and styles developed people began to say, "This Pablo Picasso is a terrific artist. He's so versatile and imaginative and gifted! He's probably a genius. Let's give him oodles of dosh for his sculptures and masses of mazuma for his paintings!"

So they did, and Pablo got richer ... and richer ... and *richer* ... and he was soon able to buy himself nice things like coal, and non-exploding sausages and luxury houses on the French Riviera. He didn't stop working though – he continued making great art until he was nearly 90 years old. "It's as if he turns his materials to gold!" marvelled his friends. It was true! When Pablo died he left behind a fortune – about six hundred million pounds (£600,000,000) – give or take the odd oodle.

Anne Girodet's bright idea – it wasn't worth a candle ... or was it?

In order to become rich, artists must know how to calculate the cost of their work. Some do it by size, others by time and materials. A-L. Girodet's method was, well, *wick*-'ed!

As Pablo Picasso discovered when he was working his night shift, it isn't easy to paint by candlelight. For a start, where do you stick the candles in order to see your work in the best possible light ... in your ears?

The French artist, Anne-Louis Girodet (1767-1824), who was actually a man, had a brilliant idea. Anne always worked at night and, in order to see what he was painting, he had a special hat made. His amazing headgear had dozens of candle-holders set into its brim. He really did have a head for lights. His hat could hold up to 40 candles and Anne-Louis Girodet, the amazing human Christmas tree, charged his customers according to how many candles he'd used during the creation of a painting.

Smellekens!

Some artists are successful for most of their career but are *always* tight-fisted, no matter how much wealth they acquire. They're even too mean to buy a candle.

The English sculptor, Joseph Nollekens (1737-1823), earned lots and lots of money from making statues and busts of famous people in 18th-century England. The celebrities of the day were prepared to pay large amounts of money to have their images carved out of stone – what a vain lot. Even though Joseph was rich, he was unbelievably mean. This is how the old skinflint saved money:

1 He sat in the dark at home so that he wouldn't have to buy candles.

2 He went round the back of his local butcher's shop and collected the scraps that had been thrown out ... then had them for his dinner.

3 He was a smuggler. Before bringing his hollow sculptures (which he'd made abroad) into England, he would first stuff them full of luxury items like expensive gloves and lace and silk stockings. The customs officers didn't suspect a thing and niggardly old Nollekens got away with paying no import taxes.

4 He always took a doggy bag with him when he went out to dinner and filled it with leftovers. The leavings weren't for his dog though – they were for him and his wife to eat later on.

5 He never lit fires in his rooms, even in the middle of winter!

6 He only ever owned one set of underwear at a time. He wore the same undies for ages and ages and just replaced them when they were worn out. Phooow! So why didn't they call him Joseph Smellekens?

So it's not really that surprising that the stingy sculptor left £200,000 when he died. This was an awful lot of money in 1823, and it still is today.

Cows ... not going cheap! Peter De Wint's system of re*moo*neration

Peter De Wint (1784-1849), the English landscape painter and art teacher, was a bit of a penny pincher who was always on the look out for money-making opportunities. One day he was watching one of his pupils draw a landscape. Peter decided that the young man's picture would be much improved if it had a few cows in it, so he painted them in for him at the edge of the picture. When the student got his bill for the lesson he was surprised to see that his money-grubbing teacher had charged him extra ... for painting in the cows!

And for this masterpiece – no charge!

Sometimes art dealers have been known to take advantage of desperately poor artists.

Gericault (1791-1824), the French horse-painter was once so broke that he couldn't afford a canvas. He was really desperate for something to paint on so he went to a dealer and said, "If you give me a blank canvas, I'll give you this finished painting of a cavalry officer on his horse!"

"But ... isn't there going to be any charge?" said the astonished dealer.

"I think they look quite nice as they are," said Gericault.

"All right!" said the dealer and he took Gericault's masterpiece, *Le Cuirassier*, in exchange for the blank canvas. He spent the rest of the day with a nagging feeling that he'd got the best of the deal!

If Gericault had hung on to that blank canvas for about 180 years, it could have made him some money, just like a similar one did for William Turnbull.

Is it a polar bear in an ice-cream storm?

The British artist, William Turnbull (1922-) entered a completely blank canvas (it was painted white all over) in the 1978 John Moores' exhibition at Liverpool. He got £3,000 pounds for it – perhaps he would have preferred a *blank* cheque.

Any colour ... as long as it's blank

Ad Rheinhardt (1913-1967) did even better with his blank canvas. He painted it black all over ... then sold it for £24,000 pounds! It put his blank balance ... in the *black*.

Ad's canvas wasn't really completely blank, nor was William's – they just looked that way if you didn't pay much attention to them. William had concentrated on creating a really interesting surface with the white paint which he'd put on his canvas. He was hoping that people would become aware of the fascinating texture of the paint, rather than just its colour.

Ad, on the other hand, was interested in colour, particularly colour that was almost colourless. His canvas was actually made up of several rectangles that were painted in varying shades of black. The people who just saw these canvases as "blank" probably missed out on an interesting visual experience – giving a few moments' careful attention to a work of art can often provide rewards that aren't always obvious at first glance. Look … look … then look again!

"I'm starving! As soon as I make some money I'm going to buy a huge piece of beef … and paint it!"

When struggling artists begin to make lots of money they don't always spend it on improving their standard of living. Chaim Soutine (1894-1943) came from a small village in Lithuania (part of Russia) and he desperately wanted to be an artist. When he was seven, he pinched his mum's best kitchen knife so he could sell it and buy crayons to draw with. When she found out she was so angry that she shut him in a cupboard in their cellar for two days.

This still didn't put Chaim off wanting to be an artist but sadly, his family were far too poor to send him to art school.

Then one day Chaim's luck changed for the better and he was beaten up by the son of the local priest. This happened because Chaim had made a drawing of the priest even though he didn't want him to.

The holy man was forced to pay Chaim's mum for the damage that his son had done to her son. So, with this money she was able to pay to have Chaim repaired and to send him to art school into the bargain.

Sadly, after he'd been to art school, Chaim was still desperately poor, even though he was a really talented and hardworking artist. This may well have had something to do with the fact that he never let anyone look at his paintings. Chaim had a morbid fear of putting his work in art exhibitions. In the hard-hearted world of art, where, believe it or not, many buyers ruthlessly ask if they can see a painting before they actually buy it – this can be a bit of a disadvantage.

So Chaim was always broke and always starving hungry and he often stood for hours at the counters of cafés in the hope that someone would take pity on him and buy him something to eat. Unfortunately though, most people went out of their way to avoid Chaim because, as well as being incredibly poor and hungry, he was also incredibly poor and dirty ... not to mention nose-shatteringly smelly.

At long last, despite all of his problems, Chaim began to earn some money from his art and he was able to buy something he'd always wanted. He bought his very first car ... cass. It was the carcass of an ox. Chaim didn't want to eat the ox – he wanted it for his art. He hung it from his studio ceiling and began to paint it. Whenever the ox began to look a bit off-colour Chaim sent his studio assistant to the local butchers for a few buckets of blood. He would then slosh the blood over the carcass to make sure it kept its "just slaughtered" appearance for the whole time he was painting it.

After a while the ox began to rot and it got extremely niffy, but being rather pongy himself, Chaim didn't seem to notice this. The local police and the health authorities did, though, and told him he had to get rid of it. Chaim begged them to allow him to keep it, saying that Art is *far* more important than trivial little matters like Public Health and sickening stenches that threaten to asphyxiate whole neighbourhoods. He did eventually finish painting the ox and it's now the star of Chaim's very famous picture entitled *The Side of Beef*. Chaim painted quite a lot of "Side of Beef" paintings. One of them is on display at the Albright Knox Gallery in Buffalo, U.S.A. (rather appropriate really).

Unforeseen expenses

As well as making money from painting, artists also have to spend it – on things like brushes, paints ... and keeping their bath water warm all day long, every day, for four months!

The British artist, John Everett Millais (1829-1896) liked to paint beautifully detailed pictures of romantic subjects. He was particularly inspired by the bit in Shakespeare's play, *Hamlet*, where a young woman called Ophelia falls into a river whilst picking flowers – silly girl – why didn't she pick them in a field? Instead of shouting for help, Ophelia then floats along the river still clutching the flowers.

John thought this charming scene would make a lovely picture so he chose a suitable river and spent the whole of the summer sitting at the side of it with his paints and easel. During all this time, not one pretty woman happened to float by clutching a bunch of flowers, so in the end John only managed to paint the river.

He decided he'd have to get a model to pose as Ophelia and he asked a young woman called Lizzie Siddal if she'd come and do a bit of floating for him. Rather than put Lizzie in the river and risk the possibility of her sinking ... or floating off and never being seen again, John thought it would be a much better idea if she came and did the floating in his bath at home.

"All right then," said Lizzie, "as long as it's warm and as long as I can keep my clothes on!"

"No problem, babe!" said John. "You can wear a lovely silver dress and I'll keep little lamps burning under the bath all the time you're in there and in that way you can simmer gently while I make my masterpiece."

John really was a stickler for detail and Lizzie had to lay in the bath for four long cold winter months while he struggled to get every tiny bit of the picture just right.

He wasn't an unreasonable man, though, and he did allow Lizzie to get out of the bath every now and again – so that her skin wouldn't go all pruney – and so that she could do all the normal things that we have to do, like going shopping and eating lunch and … having a bath.

One day when she was in John's bath Lizzy's teeth started to chatter and her skin began to turn blue.

As she walked home from John's house that evening Lizzie's nose was running so much that she could hardly keep up with it.

"Call me a doctor!" she said to her dad when she got home.

"You're a doctor!" said her dad.

This didn't make Lizzie feel any better at all so they decided to ask the local doctor to visit their house. When he arrived he told Lizzie that she had caught a cold.

"I know dat!" said Lizzie, "'ad I dough why ad well! Id's becud dat silly Billy, Mitter Millais forgod to lide de liddle lambs under de bath! Atishoo! Atishoo! Atishoo!"

After he'd fetched Lizzie three tissues and asked her why Millais was keeping sheep in his bathroom, Mr Siddal went round to the artist's house and said, "Look at this 'ere doctor's bill. It's not to be sneezed at you know! You'll 'ave to cough up for this lot mate!"

So not only did John have to pay for paints, canvases, brushes and warm baths, he also had to pay Lizzie's doctor's bill – but it was all well worth it in the end – because the painting is absolutely beautiful and has given pleasure to thousands of people since the day it was first exhibited! John's picture of Ophelia is on display at the Tate Gallery in London.

A rags to riches story

Sometimes an artist is discovered almost nightly. This next story is all about just such a discovery. **Important note**: the story takes place in the World of Art, which is inhabited by critics, dealers and collectors (and one or two artists). People who live in this alien world communicate in a special language called Arty-fficial, or Art Speak. During the story several of the characters will be talking Arty-fficial. Do not worry if you can't understand a word they are saying – they can't either!

Sometimes artists work away at their creations for years and years starving in their garret (top-floor flat), getting thinner and thinner, and smaller and smaller. Their work goes completely unnoticed for ages then, one day, they are discovered by an art critic.

99

Put some Vermeers up ... and everyone cheers up!

Not every artist is as lucky as the one in that story. Even though he had successfully completed his training as a craftsman and was considered to be a master painter, the Dutch artist, Jan Vermeer (1632-1675) had big problems finding buyers for his pictures. Jan painted exquisitely detailed and very atmospheric interior scenes, many of which feature beautifully dressed women playing musical instruments. The paintings are remarkable for the feeling of peace and calm that seems to surround them.

Part one – Neither for loaf nor money, or, life on the breadline

Jan Vermeer painted very ... very ... s-l-o-o-o-o-w-l-y and his art didn't earn enough for him and Mrs Vermeer and their eleven children to live on. Some of his pictures were actually taken away from him by his baker because Jan couldn't afford to pay his bread bills! When he died, he owed so much money that all of his 21 remaining pictures were sold to settle his debts. Even then, they didn't raise enough to pay off all that he owed. It would appear that, in 1675, no one seemed to attach much importance at all to the paintings of Jan Vermeer.

Part two – The world's longest conga
If Jan's ghost had floated over Washington, U.S.A., 321 years later in 1996, it would have seen thousands of people standing in long queues and camping out overnight in the street in freezing temperatures and raging snowstorms. So why were they queuing?

1 They were trying to get tickets to Michael Jackson's farewell comeback concert.

2 The buses were running late.

3 It was the first day of the sales.

4 They were trying to get into the *Guinness Book Of Records* for the world's longest conga dance.

It was none of these. You knew that anyway, didn't you? Read on and discover why there were queuing!

Part three – "What me? You must be joking!"
No doubt Jan's ghost would have thought ...

Just look at those poor homeless people queuing for a free hand-out of bread. I do feel sorry for them, I know just what it feels like to be unable to pay for a loaf.

He would have been entirely wrong. The thousands of people standing in the queues weren't begging – they were American art-lovers queuing overnight to get tickets to see an exhibition of just 21 of his pictures at the National Gallery.

Part four – "I want to feel all peaceful – fancy a punch-up?"

By the time of the exhibition in Washington, art lovers all over the world had made up their minds that Jan Vermeer's paintings were absolutely brilliant. They said that anyone looking at these beautiful pictures instantly felt completely calm and happy and peaceful! The tickets for the exhibition were sold out in no time at all and many thousands of people were disappointed.

During the two months that the show was open, over a third of a million people visited it. Some people in the queues were so desperate to get to see the pictures (and feel calm and peaceful) that they began to hit each other.

Art so valuable ... that it's ... priceless?

Jan's paintings are now owned by some of the wealthiest people in the world. They are said to be priceless works of art. Their owners guard them jealously and some aren't at all keen to lend them for display to the public. It took four years to persuade the Queen of England to loan hers for the exhibition in Washington.

What does it mean when an artist's work is described as being priceless?

1 It's not even worth one halfpenny.

2 The sticky bar-code ticket has fallen off and the person at the check-out has to hold the masterpiece up and shout, "Doreen, can you just find out how much the Vermeers are this week – I think they're on special offer."

3 The owner can't remember what they paid for it.

4 The picture is so mind-bogglingly valuable that no one can begin to think of what they would ask for it if they ever had to sell it.

Answer: 4. They have a value that it is impossible to calculate.

The (sad) story of Vincent Van Gogh's big break

Another Dutch artist who had problems finding buyers for his pictures was Vincent Van Gogh. He just couldn't seem to sell his paintings, despite the fact that he painted over 800 of them ... *and* had an art dealer for a brother!

Even though his work was ignored, Vincent

decided to look on the bright side. He went to live in a yellow house in the South of France, where he painted lots of cheerful subjects, like yellow furniture and yellow sunflowers and yellow ... houses! In order to continue his life as an artist Vincent was forced to live in awful poverty (what other kind is there?). At times he had nothing to eat but ship's biscuits and eggs. At one point he even ate his paints – this wasn't because they were particularly tasty – he was just fed up and trying to poison himself. Despite all of his terrible hardships Vincent carried on painting his astonishing pictures – but, alas, they still didn't sell.

Then, at long last ... after many, many long and difficult years ... things began to improve. One of Vincent's sunflower paintings was sold at Christie's Auction House in London for *twenty four million, seven hundred and fifty thousand pounds* – about two million pounds a flower. Things were definitely looking up. Suddenly, everyone wanted to own a painting by Vincent. A few months later, an Australian billionaire paid over 30 million pounds for his *Irises* picture.

Then there was even better news! His painting of his friend, Doctor Gachet, was sold for an astonishing ... *forty nine million, one hundred and seven thousand, one hundred and forty two pounds!* Sadly, though, at this point in time, Vincent had been dead for over a 100 years – and was no doubt feeling really disappointed at not having managed to be around for his big break. He could have bought an awful lot of ship's biscuits for 50 million pounds and still have enough change to buy a fleet of luxury yachts to keep them in.

Believe it or not – sunflowers really do grow on people!

Poor old Vincent felt really passionately about the things he painted. His pictures of sunflowers, irises and sun-drenched French landscapes seem to vibrate and throb with energy and colour. Unfortunately, his confident swirling brush strokes, thick layers of paint and the general feeling of excitement that comes from his paintings were all a bit much for the people of the late 19th century. They thought that his work was coarse, crude and garish.

Many years were to pass before the world in general began to appreciate what a great painter Vincent was – his energetic new style of art really did take a bit of getting used to. Nowadays people think his paintings are great. Thousands of them decorate the walls of their homes, schools and offices with prints of his pictures – or even the real thing – if they've got the odd 40 or 50 million pounds to spare!

Something special

What are works of art really worth? The actual canvases and tubes of paint that Jan and Vincent used for their paintings probably cost them just a few francs or guilders ... but wealthy art collectors eventually paid millions for the finished pictures. Was this all just because these artists had put some paint on their canvas and arranged the colours and shapes in a rather pleasing way? Well, not entirely – they had done something else as well.

With the magic touch of their brushes they had given their work a special feeling. It's probably the feeling they were experiencing when they painted the picture. It's built into every single brush stroke, the texture of the paint on the surface of the canvas and the way they've interpreted things like colour, shape, light and shadow. In some strange way this feeling is often shared by the person looking at the picture, even if the artist has been dead and gone for centuries. It stays with a great work of art forever and it's what makes it unique. It means that it can never be reproduced in exactly the same way again

– probably not even by the artists themselves. Churning out identical items is definitely *not* a job for artists – we can leave that to machines in factories.

Finishing touches

When the world wakes up to the fact that an artist has a special gift for producing work that is remarkable and unique, their art usually increases in value. In Picasso's case this happened while he was a young man and he benefited from his "golden touch" for the rest of his life. In Jan's and Vincent's case, their golden touch was only recognized long after they were dead, so they didn't get to enjoy huge financial rewards for their efforts.

Perhaps making all that great art was a reward in itself – a lot of people would pay a fortune just to have a fraction of their talent and would say they were lucky to have been so gifted. Even so, it would have been nice if they'd had a bit more recognition and success in selling their work while they were alive, wouldn't it?

Art-searching – find art for yourself!
Pablo Picasso – *Woman In a Chemise* – Tate Gallery, London
Joseph Nollekens – *Busts of the British naval heroes* – Manners, Blair and Bayne – Westminster Abbey
Peter De Wint – *The Harvest Field* – c.1840 – National Gallery of Scotland – Edinburgh

Gericault – *A Horse Frightened By Lightning* – National Gallery, London
Chaim Soutine – *Return From School After The Storm* – The Phillips Collection – Washington DC, U.S.A.
Millais – *Ophelia* – 1851-1852 – Tate Gallery
Ad Rheinhardt – *Abstract Painting No. 5* – 1962 – Tate Gallery, London
Vincent Van Gogh – *Sunflowers* – 1988 – National Gallery, London
Vermeer – *Woman Tuning a Lute* – Metropolitan Museum Of Art – New York, U.S.A.

NICKERS, PICKERS AND TRICKERS

As any millionaire art megastar would be pleased to tell you, big money can be made in the World of Art. It's not just the artists who occasionally do quite well – there are plenty of other people around who make a big profit out of the art market. Some of them do it by hard work – some by incredibly good luck – and others prefer to make it by less honest means. So is that why they become art dealers?

Don't be so disrespectful! No, of course it's not why they become art dealers ... it's why they become art dealers *and* art forgers ... like Hans van Meegeren did.

Hans Van Meegeren – the Artful Dodger (1880-1947)

Occasionally, picture dealers find themselves short of the odd masterpiece or two and they become down-'arted. They shouldn't – all they need to do is pick up their brushes and palette and get busy with a bit of "do it yourself". That's what Dutch art dealer, Hans Van Meegeren used to do. Hans was a Dutch picture seller who painted lots of counterfeit masterpieces which he then flogged to unsuspecting customers. One of his little doodles was called *Supper at Emmaus* and it fooled the art experts completely. In 1937 they described Hans's painting of Jesus and his disciples as "Vermeer's greatest achievement"!?

When it came to painting absolutely brilliant fakes, Hans was extremely handy. He even managed to pull the wool over the eyes of the German politician, Hermann Goering, when he sold him a fake Vermeer during World War Two ... then again, the ghastly, goose-stepping Goering had a trick or two up his *own* sleeve!

How handy Hans hoodwinked horrendous Hermann (and vice versa)

So all it needed now was for Hans to pay his fake money into a fake bank!

Pull the other one – it's got clogs on

After the war, one of Horrendous Hermann's collections of stolen paintings was found hidden in a salt mine (also stolen). Amongst them was the fake Vermeer he'd bought from Van Meegeren. Shortly after this the Dutch police paid a visit to Hans's house.

"What's up?" asked Hans.

"The game's up ... that's what's up, you traitor!" they cried. "Han's up, handy Hans! We are arresting you for selling art to the enemy!"

"I did not sell art to the Nazis! I tricked them – I sold them a dud! I am a loyal Dutchman. I am a forger, not a creepy collaborator!" protested Hans.

"Do you take us for dummies?" asked the Dutch authorities. "Pull the other one – it's got clogs on!"

"I am a real forger!" cried Hans. "All of my fakes are quite genuine."

"Prove it then!" demanded the authorities.

"All right then, I will!" said Hans.

He was given paints and brushes and a canvas then put in a locked and barred studio. He began work on a painting. After a while the experts took a peep to see how he was getting on. They couldn't believe what they saw! A Vermeer painting was appearing before their very eyes!

"Wow!" said the authorities. "We were wrong. You are not a fake forger – you are a real forger of genuine-fake masterpieces!"

Hans wasn't the only foxy fraudster to fool the experts...

Tricky Eric's double bluff

Eric Hebborn (1934-1996) made forgeries of paintings by artists like Sir Anthony Van Dyck (1599-1641) and Giovanni Battista Piranesi (1720-1778) (his signature must have taken some faking!). He then sold them to galleries and museums around the world. He was finally caught out when someone noticed that he'd used the same paper for work by two different artists (no, they weren't on the same piece of paper, they were just the same type of paper – he wasn't that stupid!).

After he was rumbled, Eric decided to come clean and own up to all his wrong-doings. He wrote a book about his life and in it he listed all the fakes he'd ever sold and the names of the galleries who'd bought them, but, being a born hoaxer, he couldn't resist including some pictures on the lists that weren't actually forgeries at all! He had the experts in a right old tizzy – and for a while they didn't know what was real and what was fake!

In 1996 poor Eric was found murdered in a street in Rome. Perhaps he'd been bumped off by a gang of irate art experts?

Have you got what it takes to be a foxy fraudster? Why not find out by trying the next couple of activities? You might decide the first one's a bit of a fraud after you've tried it – but you can rest assured that the second one's the genuine art-icle … honest!

Make your very own original Rembrandt – then flog it for a fortune!

The work of the great Dutch artist, Rembrandt Van Rjin (1606-1669) is mind-bogglingly valuable. Millionaire art collectors immediately reach for their cheque books whenever it comes up for auction. When he wasn't painting masterpieces, Rembrandt liked to make pen-and-ink drawings of ragged and forlorn beggars who usually looked the worse for wear and often had bits of their anatomy missing or damaged. There are probably a few of these sketches that haven't been discovered yet. If you could "create" a really good forgery of just such a drawing it would be worth a fortune on the international art market. Interested? Excited? Fancy making a cool million or three? Read on!

What you'll need

When making a forgery it is important that you stick to the materials used by the original artist. So dump that wipe-clean board and those day-glo magic markers straightaway! Rembrandt was strictly a quill and bistre man. No, this doesn't mean that Rembrandt drew with gravy – bistre is a brown pigment made from boiling soot in water. If you don't have any soot, you can use the juice from rotten apples as your substitute pigment.

So – for your junior forger's outfit you will need:

- a book containing reproductions of Rembrandt's drawings – the drawings are to study and copy in order to get a "feel" for his style – not to tear out and try and sell as genuine originals!

- some drawing paper – the older the better. Look around junk shops and second-hand book shops for this (on no account use flowery notepaper with your parents' name and address at the top – it might just give the game away!)
- a sharp knife
- an assistant – not at all sharp, preferably slightly stupid and extremely obliging
- lots of really rotten apples
- a goose, which you may well find conveniently wandering around your next requirement, which is...
- a reed bed – often found in swampy areas, but not furniture shops
- some green twigs and branches, i.e. still with the sap in
- a really good first-aid kit.

All you have to do

- Go to the reed bed and track down the goose – steal some of its feathers.
- RUN AWAY! As you and your accomplice stagger through the swamp, screaming in terror and attempting to escape the enraged goose, do your best to grab a few handfuls of reeds.

- Return home and dress your wounds with sticking plaster.
- Feeling better? Good! You're ready to work! You now have plenty of reeds and goose feathers. Trim the barbs from one of the feathers then cut off the end at an angle. Use the extra-sharp knife for this. Take your time and **be careful!** This is a tricky operation and you could well ... oops!

- Dress your new wounds with sticking plaster.
- Finish trimming and sharpening the end of your "quill". This is your pen. Do not attempt to put the goose in this pen, even if it is running around your front garden and pecking your grandmother – it's a drawing pen, remember? This is what Rembrandt made his sketches with. You now need to make a slit in the end of it with your knife this will help your apple juice ink to flow more freely. (Old scribes and artists made their reed and quill pens with pen-knives. They're still called that, even though they're used for other things.)

- Take the last rotten apple and squeeze the juice

from it. There isn't much, is there – but then again – it wasn't really a good idea to let your assistant eat the rest of the apples, was it?

- You are ready to draw. Dip your quill pen in the apple juice and start sketching. Your assistant will be your model. Start with the overall shape then put in specific details. Don't forget – this is supposed to be a drawing of a beggar by Rembrandt, so concentrate on the tragic and forlorn aspects of your subject, e.g. sick expression, peck wounds, torn and muddy clothing.

HMM... MAYBE HE LOOKS A BIT **TOO** TRAGIC AND FORLORN...

- When the drawing is finished, and your friend has stopped crying, make a fire using the green wood – the smokier the better. Hold the picture over the fire. The smoke will give it an ancient appearance, but beware – it is also extremely unpleasant and harmful – (so you could always get your friend to perform this task!).

- You are ready to sign your masterpiece – you must do this upside down. **Useful tip:** Why not save yourself the trouble of standing on your head for this operation by turning your paper upside down. Find a copy of Rembrandt's signature and turn that upside down as well. Now copy it! This is the method used by the master forgers.

Vital Tip: Rembrandt always signed the back of his drawings as well as the front. For this he

117

always used his full name which was: Rembrandt Fluffikins Sadtrousers Tinkerbell Curly Vinny Jones Van Rijn. Make sure that you do this as well and do not forget to draw the dealer's attention to it when you offer them the forgery.

Steal a famous painting – then flog it ... and flog it ... and flog it

Sometimes dodgy daubers get together with artful tea-leaves (thieves) and brew up elaborate plans for making lots of money. These plans usually involve the theft of extremely valuable paintings ... like the *Mona Lisa*. This incredibly famous painting was painted by the Italian artist, Leonardo da Vinci (1452-1519). It is a portrait of an Italian noblewoman who looks as though she is just beginning to see the funny side of a joke she was told about 400 years ago. Nowadays, such a unique art treasure would be protected from crooks by a sophisticated electronic security system, but 80 or so years ago things were different.

Le Tittle~Tattle

PARIS 1911

LAX LOUVRE LAMENTS LOSS OF LEONARDO'S LOVELY LADY

All France is stunned. Early this morning I saw grown men weeping in the boulevards of Paris. And why? Because our national treasure has disappeared. No, not our beloved Eiffel Tower ... that is still safe, thank goodness (the authorities had the good sense to padlock that to the railings – we French aren't stupid you know!). I am talking about *La Joconde* ... the *Mona Lisa*. She has disappeared, no doubt nicked by some dastardly scoundrel who snuck up on her while she wasn't looking, whisked her out of her glass case, then tucked her under their shirt and scampered off. And, because she is an ancient and noble lady, in an ancient and noble museum, there were no howls of alarm, there was no struggle, she just went quietly. Where is she now? No doubt being held prisoner in some lowly basement, being deprived of food and water. What is the world coming to? Before we know it people will be having to lock their front doors before they go to bed at night!

Correction The first line of this report should read, "Early this morning I saw grown men *sweeping* in the boulevards of Paris."

Pierre Closely – Editor – *Le Tittle Tattle*

After the *Mona Lisa* was stolen, lots of French people, who probably weren't the slightest bit interested in art, were so upset and outraged by the audacious theft that they went in their thousands to the Louvre Museum in order to stare forlornly at the bit of bare wall where the painting used to hang.

SACRE BLEU! NOW ZE BIT OF WALL WHERE ZE MONA LISA USED TO 'ANG 'AS BEEN STOLEN!

The French police were so desperate to find a culprit that they actually took Pablo Picasso in for questioning as a suspect. Perhaps they thought he had stolen her because he was jealous of Leonardo?

Not long after the theft, the *Mona Lisa* was sold by criminals to a rich American art collector ... then to another rich American art collector ... then another one ... then another... All in all, six wealthy Americans each bought the painting for 300,000 dollars. As there was only one *Mona Lisa,* how could this have happened?

1 Having sold the painting the thieves quickly re-stole it from its new owner, sure in the knowledge that they wouldn't report the theft to the police as it was already pinched and they didn't want to be prosecuted for receiving stolen goods. The gang then immediately sold it again ... then stole again ... and sold it again ... and so on!

2 The thieves made lots of colour photocopies of the original then sold them to fabulously wealthy, but

unbelievably stupid ... and short-sighted, millionaires.
3 Not long after the news of the theft hit the headlines, a gang of criminals bought up every Mona
Lisa "painting by numbers" kit they could lay their
hands on and made dozens of small children work
day and night to complete them. They chose the six
best paintings and sold them to wealthy art
enthusiasts. The rest were disposed of at car-boot
sales all over Europe.

4 Six extremely good professional fakes of the *Mona
Lisa* were painted by an expert forger and sold to art
collectors who were each told it was the stolen
original – no questions asked!

Answer: 4.
The whole thing was set up by the gang of confidence tricksters. They first organized the theft of
the real *Mona Lisa* then persuaded six rich,
American art collectors to each pay $300,000 for
what they believed was the original. What they had
actually bought were six fakes painted by the
master forger, Yves Chaudron. The wealthy Americans
obviously had more dollars than sense?

Meanwhile, the real *Mona Lisa* was at the flat of
the man who the gang had employed to steal it. He

had stolen it, first from the Louvre ... and then from them! When he tried to sell it to an Italian art dealer in 1914 he was arrested and the painting was put back in the Louvre.

Not all art thefts are brilliantly executed robberies carried out by ruthless professional master minds.

More "moving" stories
Quick! follow that bus!
In 1989 a drunken man walked into the Birmingham City Art Gallery and took the painting *The Death of Chatterton* off the wall. He then carried the £25,000-worth of art out into the street and made his escape ... on a double-decker bus!

Goering ... Goering ... gone!
Horrid Hermann Goering was a slightly more ambitious art thief than the man in Birmingham. Instead of being content to pinch just one picture he swiped five thousand, two hundred and eighty one of them! He was probably the greediest art thief the world has ever seen.

With a little help from his pestilential pal, awful Adolf (Hitler), hateful Hermann wandered into museums and galleries all over Europe and helped himself to any art that took his fancy, including masterpieces by Rembrandt, Rubens (1577-1640) and Goya (1746-1828). By the end of World War Two, the nasty Nazi may well have been running a bit short of wall space on which to hang his pillaged pics! He probably wasn't too bothered anyway, he certainly didn't seem to have much affection for the wonderful art he'd stolen.

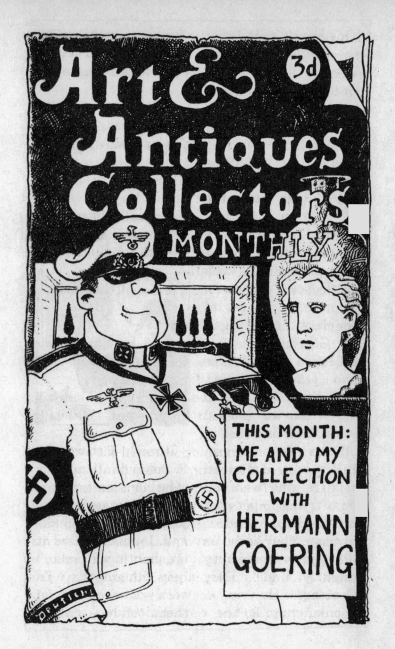

This issue's collector of the month is a Mr H. Goering of Nazi Germany. Mr Goering has a really fabulous collection of European masterpieces which he keeps at various locations ... like his heavily fortified villa ... and his heavily fortified salt mine. We visited the villa, having first promised to keep its location a secret. Apparently, a lot of people want to talk to Mr Goering about his collection (and one or two other matters). In fact, on our way to his villa we passed some British artillery officers and several thousand American soldiers who were all busy trying to get past a German Panzer division. They asked us if we knew where they might find Herr Goering. He *is* a popular chap, isn't he –

surely they can't *all* be wanting to do interviews for art magazines ... can they?

Well, we finally arrived at Goering Towers and, when we'd got past the massive, slavering rottweilers ... and the massive, slavering S.S. men ... we were shown around Mr Goering's Art collection.

It really is enormous! It contains thousands of brilliant masterpieces by painters like Rembrandt, Rubens and Goya. As I gazed at the paintings I couldn't help thinking that I'd seen quite a few of them before – on the walls of museums all over Europe, actually. When I ventured to mention this to Mr Goering he became somewhat annoyed and ordered some S.S. men to take me to his cellar where they chained me to the wall and tortured me mercilessly for the rest of that afternoon.

So, later in the evening, as the storm-troopers were helpfully carrying my stretcher around the last bit of the collection, I decided not to refer to the matter again.

As I was leaving Goering Towers, the American and British art enthusiasts I was telling you about earlier had just arrived and were engaged in hand-to-hand combat with the Rottweilers and the S.S. men. At this point Herr Goering suddenly seemed to go off art and began to make hurried preparations to burn the whole of his collection.

In next month's issue we'll be talking to a Mr A Hitler of Berlin about his unusual hobby of collecting other people's countries and we'll be taking a peek at his interesting but rapidly dwindling collection.

As soon as he realized the allies were definitely going to win the war he cold-heartedly began making plans to destroy the entire hoard! Fortunately he was captured before he could get round to it, so he destroyed himself instead by committing suicide. The paintings were then returned to their rightful owners ... but were they?

Whose art is it anyway?

For some strange reason Hermann actually considered his knocked-off art to be his personal property. In other words, he thought he was the rightful owner, although it is perfectly obvious to everyone else that he wasn't. Sometimes the question of who actually owns a piece of art can be quite complicated, especially if it is ancient art that was removed from another country a long time ago.

In the days when European countries were building their empires and colonizing other bits of the world, many of the early explorers and adventurers were fond of bringing little souvenirs back from their travels – like a couple of thousand slaves, or the entire contents of an Egyptian pyramid. The Spaniards were rather keen on art works made from gold and silver by the ancient Incas of Peru and brought large quantities home with them – having first killed off the original owners.

When the British and French were discovering the treasures of the ancient pyramids they thought it was perfectly alright to "borrow" artefacts – which they often forgot to return! So it's quite possible that one or two important British art collections contain items that should never be there in the first place. This removal of ancient art from its country of origin occasionally leads to international tiffs and squabbles.

Can we have our marbles back please?

In the early 19th century the Earl of Elgin "acquired" some marbles from the Greeks. Not in a toff's game of marbles in the playground – these marbles are sculptures which used to stand in the Ancient Greek temple known as the Parthenon. The Earl of Elgin came along and "acquired" them, then "exported" them back to England. Greece was ruled by the Turks at the time so the poor old Greeks didn't really get much of a chance to say whether they wanted them to go or not. The Earl obviously thought the whole thing was a great idea, especially as he eventually sold the sculptures to the British Museum for £35,000 (a really massive sum of money in those days).

The sculptures are now known as the Elgin marbles. The Greeks desperately want them back but the British Museum reckons they're theirs because they've paid for them. Occasionally the Greek and British governments have a really lively playground squabble over who actually owns the marbles ... then burst into tears and rush off to tell their mums about the whole thing.

It's surprising that the Greeks haven't considered "acquiring" and "exporting" some ancient British art themselves, as a way of getting their own back. There must be something ancient lying around somewhere that they can "borrow"? What about ... that heap of rubble on Salisbury Plain. No one would miss that – would they? Just imagine the newspaper headlines!

STONEHENGE KIDNAPPED BY GREEKS

"WE'LL DO YOU A SWAP!" SAY GREEKS, "GIVE US BACK OUR ANCIENT MARBLES ... AND WE'LL GIVE YOU BACK YOUR ANCIENT DOMINOES!"

Some people don't have to steal art – they're just rich enough to buy it whenever it takes their fancy. These wealthy collectors go to amazing lengths to get their hands on the art that is so very close to their heart.

How to track down your very own masterpiece

It can be a tough and confusing life being a mega-rich art collector. William Randolph Hearst was a phenomenally successful newspaper publisher who lived in California. He kept his enormous collection of art in his gigantunormous mansion, which he modestly called Hearst Castle.

One day, William was looking through an old magazine when he spotted a photograph of a fabulous work of art made from silver. He immediately fell in love with the silver masterpiece and said, "I've got to have that!" He thought that it was probably somewhere in England so he quickly telephoned his representative there and told her to track it down and buy it for him. After making long and painstaking enquiries the woman contacted him to say that she was completely unable to trace it. William was not a man who gave up easily. He hired a private detective and said, "Find that piece of art at all costs ... I must have it!"

The super sleuth left no stone unturned in his quest for the silver and he was eventually able to report back to William and tell him that he'd been successful in locating its whereabouts.

He had bought the silver six years earlier, then forgotten all about it. It was still in its packing case at Hearst Castle. Did he make himself a really good offer for it now that he knew who the owner was?

Art mad ... or what?

If art enthusiasts like William Randolph Hearst didn't exist, the dealers – and maybe the forgers and thieves as well – would soon be out of a job. They all depend on the mysterious and peculiar passion that so many humans have for art. There's no doubt about it – lots of people are art mad – they must be ... just look at the way they've flocked to the big exhibitions.

- In 1994 over **two hundred and ninety-six thousand** people went to see the Picasso exhibition at the Tate Gallery.
- In 1974 over **seven hundred and seventy-one thousand** people went to see an exhibition of Chinese Art at the Royal Academy.
- In 1995 **seven thousand people** queued to see Damien Hirst's half-a-cow and half-a-calf at the Tate Gallery (were the tickets half-price?).
- In 1972 over **one million, six hundred and ninety-four thousand** people went to see the Tutankhamun exhibition of Ancient Egyptian art

130

at the British Museum (not all at the same time, though!).

So it's true, people really do love looking at art ... and if they can afford it, they also buy it. But why spend so much money on it? After all, you can't eat it, you can't wear it, and you can't drive it down the street. So why buy it?

The Awful Art survey – why do people collect art?

Some customers in a well known art gallery were asked what they were spending their money on ... and why. Here are some of their replies:

131

THIS ARTIST IS THE BEST THING SINCE SLICED MUESLI AND IS DESTINED TO BE A MEGASTAR. I RECOMMEND YOU BUY THIS PICTURE IMMEDIATELY. IT'S THE WORK OF A GENIUS.... ALL RIGHT THEN, YES, I **DID** PAINT IT!

NORMAN'S RETIRING AT THE END OF THE MONTH SO ME AND THE LADS ARE BUYING HIM THIS PICTURE OF A MAN BEING MENACED BY A PACK OF WOLVES TO REMIND HIM OF ALL THE HAPPY YEARS HE'S SPENT WORKING AS A POSTMAN

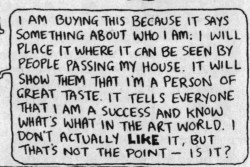

I AM BUYING THIS BECAUSE IT SAYS SOMETHING ABOUT WHO I AM: I WILL PLACE IT WHERE IT CAN BE SEEN BY PEOPLE PASSING MY HOUSE. IT WILL SHOW THEM THAT I'M A PERSON OF GREAT TASTE. IT TELLS EVERYONE THAT I AM A SUCCESS AND KNOW WHAT'S WHAT IN THE ART WORLD. I DON'T ACTUALLY **LIKE** IT, BUT THAT'S NOT THE POINT — IS IT?

I CAN'T RESIST THREE-TOED SLOTHS. I'VE GOT THE BIGGEST COLLECTION OF SLOTHABILIA IN EAST FRIMLEY. THAT'S WHY I'M BUYING THIS POST-CARD REPRODUCTION OF LEONARDO'S **'EVE AND THE THREE-TOED SLOTH BEING EXPELLED FROM PARADISE'** ISN'T IT JUST THE CUTEST LITTLE SLOTH YOU EVER DID SEE? AND HAVE YOU NOTICED THE WAY THE EYES SEEM TO FOLLOW YOU AROUND THE ROOM?

After all this reading about art you want to become a collector yourself.

Starting your own art collection

"I'd like to be an art collector!" you might say. "But I can't afford it – I'm still paying off the bank loan I took out to buy my designer trainers!" Do not despair, oh ye of little pocket money! It is possible to buy art quite cheaply. Why not search around:

- Junk shops, car-boot sales, jumble-sales, flea-markets – you'd be surprised at the snips that are to be had here, and often for as little as 10 or 20 pence – it's just a matter of using your eyes and driving a hard bargain. And you never know ... if you're really lucky you might also take home the odd flea!

- Your own attic – some people do actually stumble across lost art treasures in their attics.

So get searching right away, but remember, attics are dangerous places – you may need an adult to help you.

> **WARNING!**
> FOR FLAT DWELLERS – IF YOU ARE SEARCHING YOUR ATTIC FOR ART AT THIS MOMENT – STOP! THIS IS NOT YOUR ATTIC – IT IS THE FLAT OF THE PEOPLE UPSTAIRS AND YOU HAVE JUST STOLEN THEIR BEST TEA SERVICE!

- Auctions (sales where art is sold to whoever offers the most money)

A lot of art is sold at auctions and people who buy at them occasionally pick up a painting that turns out to be a bit of a bargain. An art dealer called Philip Parker went to a sale held by Sotheby's, the well-known art auctioneers. A painting caught his attention and he bought it for £180. He put the picture into another sale which was being held by Christie's, the other well-known art auctioneers. The painting was sold again, but for slightly more than Philip had paid for it at the first auction – £380,000 to be exact.

So between the two auctions Philip had made himself a tidy little profit of over a third of a million pounds – just by being very, very observant ... and knowing a lot about art! The painting he had spotted turned out to be an important portrait of a pope, by the Renaissance artist, Piombo. Philip obviously has a nose for this kind of bargain – his friends in the art trade don't call him "Nosey Parker" though, he's actually known as the "Hoover" (because he manages to "pick up" lots of bargains).

Important note: If you are thinking of attending an art auction do not raise your hand to ask to go to the loo while the sale is on – or you may find that you have just bought the entire contents of an Edwardian country mansion!

- Another way to buy bargain art is to discover an up-and-coming, but struggling, artist who is willing to sell their work cheaply – you never know – there might even be someone in your school or street who will eventually become the Picasso of the 21st century. The trick is to spot their talent early and get in with an offer quickly before they hit the big time. The budding superstar may not even want cash for their work, they might be happy to do a swap for some football cards or some sweets.

"I can't be bothered waiting until I grow up – I think I'll be famous right now!"

If Alexandra Nichita had been at your school and you were thinking of buying one of her paintings while she was a struggling, unknown artist you would have to have been very quick with your offer. Alexandra, who was born in Romania in 1986, now lives in Los Angeles. Since her family moved to America her career has developed rather rapidly!

- When Alexandra was two she started drawing with pen and ink.
- When she was five she moved to something a bit more challenging and began painting with watercolours.

135

- When she was eight she had an exhibition of her work at the local library and people thought it was great.

- By the time she was nine Alexandra had a total of seven one-girl exhibitions of her brightly-coloured, dream-like pictures at proper art galleries.
- By the time she was ten she had sold 200 of her paintings.
- Collectors had paid over two and a half million pounds for her work.
- Alexandra's paintings sell for about one hundred thousand dollars each and she has a waiting list of collectors wanting her work.

Some of the American buyers obviously really liked Alexandra's paintings. Others may have just seen them as a "good investment" and hoped they'd eventually be worth even more than the $100,000 they paid for them. There's nothing to guarantee that the prices will go on rising. Some artists do actually go out of fashion and their work is eventually ignored by the art world. Sometimes the prices of pictures actually fall. It's a risky business investing in art – especially if you don't have the money to pay for it in the first place...

Mr Bond's high-risk irises

An Australian businessman called Alan Bond decided that he'd like to own Vincent Van Gogh's famous *Irises* painting. So he borrowed some money then paid over £30 million for the picture at an auction. Unfortunately, Alan got into debt and was unable to make the final payment on his loan. He was forced to sell the picture to the American billionaire art collector, J. Paul Getty, who got it for the knock-down price of £25 million (a real giveaway). It might be easier to explain this arrangement in mathematical terms, so, £30,000,000 – £25,000,000 = Ouch! (if you're Mr Bond) ... or = Mmm! Very nice! (if you're Mr Getty).

Finishing touches

Perhaps the best way for people to buy art is to first of all make sure that they like it, then to make sure they can afford it – that way they will enjoy it. If it does happen to become very valuable then that's an added bonus – well, as long as their beloved works of art don't turn out to be stolen ... or forged!

Art-searching – find art for yourself!
Van Meegeren – *Supper at Emmaus* – Museum Boymans, Rotterdam, Holland
Rembrandt Van Rjin – *Beggar Leaning On a Stick* – Rijksmuseum, Amsterdam, Holland
Leonardo da Vinci – *Mona Lisa* – Louvre, Paris
The Elgin Marbles – British Museum, London

HERE'S SOME THEY MADE EARLIER...

Art collectors on the lookout for a bargain would be extremely jealous of the job lot of art treasures that were snapped up by the American explorer, John Lloyd Stephens in 1839. He bought a whole city full of art ... for just a few dollars! John and his artist pal, Frederick Catherwood were exploring the forests of Central America when they discovered the site of the lost city of Copan, which had been built thousands of years earlier by the ancient people known as the Mayas. The man who owned the site thought it was worthless ... so he sold it to John for just $50!

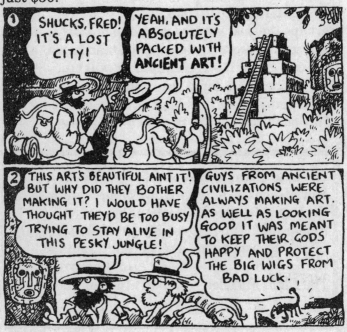

Fred was right – Art was really important in all the ancient civilizations. The powerful rulers of most early societies quickly discovered that artists could be extremely useful people to have around – especially if they'd got problems with stroppy gods!

Extracts from my diary by
An Ancient ruler

SUNNYDAY 12th, 64,005,000 A.D. (AFTER DINOSAURS)

What a lovely day! The sun has been shining, the dodos have been singing and the spaghetti crop is flourishing. The gods are happy and all is well with the world!

WOESDAY 13th

Oh disaster, disaster, disaster! (PTO)

Disaster! The gods are angry! Someone (me?!?) forgot to bow down to them 300 times before bedtime and during the night they sent a troupe of clog-dancing hippopotamuses to cavort all over the spaghetti fields as a punishment. Our crops are ruined! We will starve to death! How on earth can we make the gods happy again?

GLOOMDAY 14TH

Offered the gods two crispy-fried water buffalo and a six-pack of slaves along with a little note which said "Sorry about the bowing." Still not happy! They say they had savoury slaves in breadcrumbs last week and if we can't do better than that they'll light the blue touchpaper on the big volcano and cover us all in red-hot larva! They've given us 2 days to come up with some really original gift ideas that will make them ecstatically happy — **OR ELSE!**

What are we to do?

WORSEDAY 15TH

Things are getting worse! Guess what the high priest has just offered the God of the Sea... only a prawn cocktail! Would you believe it? I mean we're only talking about the **god** who created the **whole** Indian Ocean in one afternoon! No wonder he's feeling insulted! Can't say I blame him! MEMO TO SELF: Feed high priest to Sharks as a Sacrifice to Sea God - that'll teach him!

DOOMDAY 16TH

24 hours to go! Mustn't panic. Must do some hard thinking! What we need are some gifts that will really amaze the gods. Something special. Something they couldn't make. It's a difficult one, is this. After all, they made the whole world didn't they... and us humans to boot!

What we need is something completely original... and beautiful. Something that they couldn't have thought of or created themselves. That's it! Of Course! What we need is "that Something Special for the god who has everything!" I think I'll have a word with the artisans!

GOODAY 17TH

Oh joy oh joy oh joy! We're Saved! The artisans worked all through the night and this morning we've presented the gods with the most beautiful creations imaginable. They're over the moon! The sun's shining again, the spaghetti is sprouting and the dodo is singing! (All the others got squashed by the hippos. Even this one's looking a bit off-colour!)

141

There was lots of art around in ancient civilizations and much of it was made for the gods. Even someone who has stayed on at school for a long time – like a professor – doesn't understand everything about it. He would need to talk to an ancient artist to discover the secrets of his trade...

Three-thousand-year-old secrets revealed at last – ancient artist tells all

Artist – Listen! Us artists, or artisans, as we were called in those days, had the talent and skill and in some cases, the genius (looks smug) to make things that were stunning and awe-inspiring and gorgeous to behold. We created beautiful temples for the gods to live in ... and paintings ... and sculptures which said ...

We think you gods are absolutely divine, and this is our way of telling you.

Professor: Talking sculptures! Wow!

Artist: No, just dumb ones (a bit like you really). We weren't Walt Disney you know! We tried our very best because we knew that the more magnificent a particular piece of art was, the happier the god would be, and, in that way, some really wonderful and beautiful things were made. We also knew that the gods were really vain, so we made flattering portraits and statues of them as well.

Professor: (*astonished*) But how did you know what the gods looked like if they were mostly invisible?

Artist: (*grinning*) Us artists knew exactly what the gods and goddesses looked like. We've got special magical, visionary powers (winks at professor). Not to mention fabulous imaginations ... ay ... ay? (*Elbows professor in ribs, laughs and winks again*). Anyway, some gods were a piece of cake – like the Ancient Egyptian cat goddess! I made her. She was a doddle.

CAT GODDESS, GUV'NOR? NO WORRIES – I'LL JUST WHIP THE TOP OFF A SPHINX AND BANG A CAT'S HEAD ON... I'LL HAVE IT READY TUESDAY.

Professor: A doodle?

 Artist: No, a *doddle*! She was easy – she looked just like...

143

Professor: A cat?

Artist: Exactly! So all I had to do was make a big hollow moggy, fill it with a few old pussy bones, put it in the temple and in no time at all the real Cat Goddess would be purring with delight and grinning like a ... Cheshire cat!? The rulers and the people were well impressed. When they saw our portraits of the gods they thought what a god, sorry, good likeness we had managed to get and said, "This is so like the real thing that we might as well bow down and worship it, especially now that the divine spirit of the god has magically entered it."

Professor: (*all excited*) Which explains why so many ancient works of art are found in temples and other places of worship. Well I never! I've

spent years wondering why that was. I'll just rush off and write this all down. By the way ... how many 'z's are there in "artisan"?

WELL, REALLY! MY NOSE ISN'T **THAT** BIG!

AND HE'S MADE ME LOOK **REALLY FAT!**

Not all ancient art was made for the gods. Some was created to ensure that the rulers had a good time in the next world...

PROBLEM PAGE

"Dear Auntie Nefertiti

I am a pharaoh and my life is one long rave-up. I live in the lap of luxury and I am waited on all day long by grovelling lackeys. I want for nothing. So you may be asking, "Why write to a problem page?"   Well, Auntie, I do have two big worries, which are:

1 What's going to happen to my squillionaire life-style when I pop my flip-flops - you know - when I'm D.E.A.D?

The last thing I want to do is turn up in the Next Life and find I haven't got my favourite comfy throne with me, or my most grovelly servant! **The After-Life just won't be worth living!**

2 When I arrive on the other side, what will I do about...personal freshness... you know... underarm rot! I mean, how's a chap expected to strut his stuff in the Next World when he's rapidly turning into a foul-smelling blob of decaying flesh? I'm an important man around these parts— I dread to think what will happen if one of the gods tries to shake hands with me!

Yours sincerely
Worried of Thebes

145

And here's the reply

Dear Worried of Thebes

Don't fret so luvvie - there isn't a problem! All
you have to do is get some of those ever so
artistic artisan chappies to paint pictures
of scenes from your brilliant life all over
your tomb walls. This way the gods of the
Next World will know that you are a really
happening and groovy kind of Pharaoh.

If you threaten the artisans nicely they will
also paint portraits of your favourite servants
and girlfriends at no extra charge. The moment
you arrive in the After-Life the pictures will
miraculously come to life and before you can
say "Tut's your Uncle!" the slaves will be
serving up fig rolls and asses' milk shakes
while you and the girls bop away like there's
no tomorrow (which, of course, there won't
be!)

Regarding the delicate matter of personal
decay- don't fret! Just wrap up well for the
journey to the Next World and everything
will be fine. I can recommend an excellent
mobile mummyfiying service! I promise you,
you won't be disappointed _ you'll be
pickled to death!

And just to make sure that your handsome
mush is reincarnated perfect in every detail
(I'm sure you'll want to look your best for
all eternity) why not get an artisan to
paint your portrait right away... then
pop it in your tomb?

Will you do that for me luvvie?
Happy rebirthday
Auntie Nefertiti

The story of the Duke of Hamilton's feet

The Duke of Hamilton was a rich English aristocrat who was wild about Ancient Egyptian Art. He really admired the way the pharaohs lived – and he was absolutely nuts about the way they died!

He decided that he would like nothing more than to be buried in the style of an Egyptian Pharaoh (but only when he was dead – of course!). In order to prepare for his Egyptian-style D.I.Y. funeral he bought himself a beautiful and incredibly expensive ancient Egyptian stone coffin – a sarcophagus – and some embalming fluid with which to preserve his body after death.

Eventually the Duke fell ill and, as he lay dying, his servants measured him for his new home. They were dismayed to find that he was too long for the sarcophagus ... by exactly two feet ... the kind with toes and bunions, that is! When he was told that he'd been sold short the Duke was furious, but, knowing that he wasn't long for the world of the living, he pointed to the sarcophagus and cried, "Double me up in it!"

NOT **NOW**, YOU IDIOT! WAIT TILL I'M **DEAD**!

Eventually the Duke died and was successfully buried in his stone coffin. So, how did the servants solve the problem? Did they?

1 Fold him double inside the sarcophagus, just like he'd commanded them to.

2 Dump his body in a lake and sell the sarcophagus to the British Museum.

3 Cut off his feet so that the rest of him fitted the sarcophagus – then bury the feet in a mini-coffin all of their own.

4 Bury him standing up with his head sticking out of the top of the sarcophagus, but with a woolly hat on in case it got a bit nippy at nights.

Answer: 3. He entered the after life footloose and fancy free!

Awful ancient art – fab finds
Arthur Povey's piffling trifle

Sometimes people own items of ancient art and don't even know they've got them. Mr Arthur Povey spent years eating trifle from his favourite dish without realizing that it was worth a fortune (the dish – not the trifle!)

Mr Povey was completely bowled over when the dish was eventually sold for *seventeen thousand, eight hundred and fifty pounds!*

Three useful tips from an art expert

- You too could be eating your shredded wheat from a valuable ancient relic. It could be worth a fortune! Check the writing on the bottom immediately.

- What a mess! Next time – finish your breakfast before you turn the bowl over.

- Look at the label! If it says, "Ancient Chinese pottery (Shang dynasty 1750 B.C.). This item is not dishwasher-proof" – prepare for a disappointment.

Plunging to their tomb

In 1990 an American tourist was riding his horse through the desert near El Ghiza in Egypt when the horse suddenly disappeared ... closely followed by the American. They had both plunged through the soft sand into an ancient Egyptian tomb which no one had previously known about (apart from the people who made it of course). When a rescue party went into the tomb they found a rare and priceless 4,400-year-old, eight-and-a-half-inch (about 20 cm) high statuette ... and an American with a horse!

You and whose army? – Emperor Di's inaction men

Some ancient art finds are bewilderingly awesome – and awesomely bewildering! A Chinese emperor called Quin Shi Huang Di got his artists to make 7,000 life-sized model soldiers for him. Each soldier has its own individually recognizable face, hands

and uniform. It is probably the biggest and best collection of Action Men the world has ever seen! Well, "Inaction" Men really ... they haven't moved for the last 2,000 years. The soldiers are called the "Terracotta Army" (because they're made from red clay) and were discovered by some Chinese villagers digging a well.

We don't know whether or not the Emperor gave his clay figures names ... or even got round to playing with them. This wasn't really what he'd had them made for. Apparently, the real reason he had the soldiers created was to protect him ... when he was dead! They were made to go in his tomb!

What a good idea! That's just what everyone needs when they're dead, isn't it ... a load of soldiers to save their ... life! What on earth *did* Quin Shi Huang Di want the soldiers to protect him from ... worms?

This idea of the Emperor's might seem extremely ridiculous to us. But we live in the late 20th century

OI! YOU WORMS! DON'T YOU KNOW THAT'S AN ANCIENT CHINESE EMPEROR YOU'RE NIBBLING? HOP IT!

SORRY!

and we've got T.V.s and cars and computers and quite a few of us *think* we know what's what. Two thousand years ago people had very different ideas and beliefs. Quin Shi Huang Di really did think that these clay models would somehow protect him, or his spirit, in the afterlife ... and if you'd tried to tell him he was wrong he would have told his real troops to turn you into minced morsels.

Two characters from the Ancient World who did see slightly more action than Emperor Di's terracotta army were the painters, Zeuxis and Parhassius. One day these two deadly rivals decided to hold a contest to discover which of them was the most skilful artist...

Make my day ... draw!

1. THE TIME: ANCIENT THE PLACE: GREECE

I AM THE MOST WONDERFUL PAINTER IN ANCIENT GREECE!

2. WELL YOU'RE WRONG THERE PARRHASIUS. FOR A START, WE'RE NOT EVEN **IN** ANCIENT GREECE!

3. WE'RE IN **MODERN** GREECE! IT'LL ONLY BE CALLED **ANCIENT** GREECE WHEN MANY CENTURIES HAVE GONE BY!

4. ANYWAY, **I** AM THE MOST DEVASTATING DAUBER AROUND THESE PARTS: **EVERYONE** KNOWS THAT!

5. SHUCKS, ZEUXIS — THERE'S ONLY ONE WAY TO SETTLE THIS... WE'LL HAVE OURSELVES A LITTLE OLD **PAINT OUT!**

6. YOU'RE ON, PARRHASIUS! GO FOR YOUR BRUSHES AND **DRAW!**

7 ZEUXIS USED HIS SKILL TO CREATE A BEAUTIFUL PICTURE OF SOME GRAPES

HOW'S ABOUT THAT THEN?

WOW! IT'S CERTAINLY VERY IMPRESSIVE!

8 THEY WERE SO REALISTIC THAT A BIRD FLITTED DOWN TO PECK AT THEM.

SPLATCH!

OW! CAW! THEY CERTAINLY HAD ME FOOLED!

9 WELL I THINK THAT JUST ABOUT PROVES I'M THE TOPS. NOW WHERE'S YOUR EFFORT?

RIGHT HERE

10 TSSK! YOU CAN'T BE FEELING VERY CONFIDENT ABOUT YOUR PICTURE IF YOU'VE HAD TO HIDE IT BEHIND THIS TATTY OLD CURTAIN! LET'S HAVE A LOOK AT IT!

11 WHAT?! THERE'S NO CURTAIN THERE! ONLY THE SURFACE ON WHICH PARRHASIUS HAS PAINTED HIS PICTURE... **OF A CURTAIN!**

SCRABBLE

SCRABBLE

12 WOW, PARRHASIUS, THAT'S INCREDIBLE! YOU REALLY ARE THE BEST ARTIST IN ANCIENT GREECE!

MY BEAK HURTS!

It is obvious from this story that Parrhasius certainly knew how to draw the curtains. He definitely had the final chuckle in this encounter, but in another episode, it was Zeuxis who had the last laugh. An old woman came to him and asked him if he'd paint her a picture of Aphrodite, the beautiful Greek Goddess of Love. Zeuxis agreed but then the woman, who was very wrinkled and extremely ancient, said that she would be the model for the painting.

You could have knocked old Zeuxis down with a feather but nevertheless he began the painting. He was tickled pink by the idea and all the time he was painting he kept thinking how silly it was that he should be attempting to make this wrinkled old person look like a beautiful young goddess. Eventually, he could contain himself no longer and he burst out laughing. He laughed so hard that he died. (Moral: he who laughs last ... drops dead.)

155

Finishing touches
Ancient arty-fact
Ancient, all-powerful and fabulously wealthy rulers ordered artists to make wonderful works of art. The rulers then had these beautiful creations buried in sealed underground chambers. These chambers are known as tombs. The works of art remained hidden away for years and years without anyone seeing or enjoying them.

Modern arty-fact
Modern all-powerful and wealthy art collectors pay vast sums of money for wonderful works of art. The collectors then have these beautiful creations sealed in underground chambers. These chambers are known as bank vaults and museum storage areas. The works of art remain hidden away for years and years without anyone seeing them or enjoying them.

Art-searching – find art for yourself!
Banquet Scene painted on stucco c 1400 B.C. – From The Tomb of Netamun, Thebes, Egypt, British Museum, London.
Portrait Of The Princess Neferti-abet – painted on limestone slab *c*. 2500 B.C. and taken from royal burial ground Giza, Egypt – Louvre Museum, Paris, France.

AWFUL ART – OR IS IT?

Now that you've discovered a bit more about art, do you think you would know:

- How to recognize a piece of "good" art?
- How to recognize a piece of "bad" art?
- How to recognize that something is *actually* art?

At times people have violent disagreements about art – they have even been known to hit each other to prove a point. Art really does get human beings hot under the collar, especially if it's abstract ... or if it's made from unusual or unconventional materials ... or if it's rude!

How people react to art that is "out of the ordinary"

- If they're really polite they say ...

Mmmm that's different?

but they might well be thinking ...

What a total pile wombat's doings! – I wouldn't have that heap of bilge in my house if the artist paid me a million pounds!

- If they're really posh they might say,

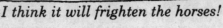

I think it will frighten the horses!

    (Though what they're doing showing art to horses
… is anyone's guess!)

- If they aren't particularly posh, or polite, they
  might just jump up and down, gnashing their
  teeth and foaming at the mouth and yelling,

*What a load of codswallop – it's absolutely
disgusting. What's it supposed to be when it's at
home anyway. My three-year-old could do better
than that!*

    (And that's just the frame!)

Someone else might say, "It's brilliant art! The rest
of you are just a load of ignoramuses!"

Jack the Dripper strikes again ... and again ... and again!

Jackson Pollock (1912-1956) was an artist whose
paintings like *Untitled* (1948) and *Number 30*
(1950) made some people tingle with pleasure ...
and others really see red (plus lots of other colours).

    Jackson was a New York-based American painter
who did actually use conventional materials for his
paintings – but he used them in a very unconventional way. Jackson was an abstract

expressionist. This meant that rather than painting nudes round the door, he expressed his feelings with paint and created pictures made up of shapes, patterns and forms that didn't actually look like anything you might recognize. In other words his pictures are a mass of multi-coloured drips, splashes, splatters, streaks and dollops ... with a few spectacular splodges thrown in for good measure (literally!)

You might well be thinking, "So what? What's so wonderful about that? If you want to see that kind of thing why not just take a look at my baby brother's nappy?" But for some strange reason Jackson's paintings are very attractive and compelling. Lots of people, who like other more conventional kinds of art as well, think so too, and go to see the paintings in their thousands.

You might also be thinking that Jackson's pictures would have been dead easy to forge. After all – any idiot can make splodgy, scribbly streaks all over a piece of canvas ... can't they? And one splodgy mess looks like another ... doesn't it? Well, not really. During the 1960s, a few years after Jackson had been killed in a car crash and when his paintings were beginning to sell for thousands of dollars, some other people had the same idea. They tried to paint and sell Pollock look-alikes (Pollookalikes?) but the forgeries were spotted very quickly. This was probably because Jackson's pictures had a special something about them – an unmistakable quality that only he could give them.

Perhaps he had an inimitable splodging action or an unrepeatable splattering style – just like fast bowlers or darts players and other sports stars have their own unique action? Even though Jackson Pollock was teasingly nicknamed "Jack the Dripper" when he was alive, many people now consider him to have been an artistic genius.

Give it the action, Jackson!

When Jackson began a picture he would first lay a very big canvas on the floor. He then opened a big can of paint and began to pour it down a stick onto the canvas. As soon as the canvas was well-covered he would start to hurl and flick and drip other colours on top. Sometimes, in order to give the painting an interesting texture he liked to mix sand or broken glass into the thick layers of paint that were covering the canvas.

If he got really carried away and was short of materials he would grab anything that came to hand, like the tops from the tubes of his oil paints, or drawing pins and nails that happened to be lying around the studio. He even dug into his pockets for bits and bobs to add to the wet paint. Things like keys, buttons, bus tickets, coins, cigarette ends and matches all ended up as part of the picture.

Monstrous materials

Safety-pins and cigarette-ends aren't really what people think of as art materials, are they? Jackson wasn't alone in his fondness for making art out of any odd bits and pieces he could lay his hands on. While many artists are actually quite content to use traditional materials like paper and clay, others go out of their way to find something new and original to turn into a work of art. The weirder the better in many cases...

Five of the following examples of unusual art materials are genuine – one is deliberately untrue – it's so silly you'd have to be an idiot not to spot it!

1 The handlebars and saddle of a bicycle. Pablo Picasso used these items to make a sculpture of a bull's head (*shortly afterwards he was involved in a mysterious cycling accident*).

2 A heap of bricks. The sculptor, Carl André, exhibited a pile of bricks at the Tate Gallery. Large numbers of the public were outraged by this exhibit but it was a great inspiration to builders' merchants everywhere. Many of them were so impressed with Carl's masterpiece that they created exact copies of it on building sites throughout the land.

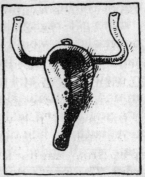

3 The cast-off skin of a boa constrictor snake, some drawing-pins and an old school desk. Swedish artist, Lars Dieter Olsen, featured this exhibit in his show at the Hayward Gallery in 1972. He pinned the snakeskin to the desk lid and called it

"Rictus". He said it symbolized the struggle of the artist to escape the awful effects of his education.

4 The bears at Chessington Zoo, some bear food and some food dye. The artist, Peter Kuttner, coloured the bear food with the dye then fed it to the bears. Then what did he do? Well ... nothing really, apart from calling this art event, *The Edible Rainbow*.

5 Five hundred pounds of potatoes. A South American artist, Victor Grippo, set out 500 pounds of potatoes in an art gallery in Birmingham. He then pushed a small connector into each one and linked the whole lot to a machine that measured electrical output. He said that his exhibit was meant to symbolize hidden talents. A lot of people thought that Victor's talents were also hidden.

6 A large mountain in America and a lot of elbow grease. (Your teacher will tell you what elbow grease is – there are probably several tins of it in the caretakers'

cupboard.) Gutzon Borglum carved the heads of Presidents Washington, Jefferson, Lincoln and Roosevelt into the side of Mount Rushmore. Each head is 60 feet high (about 28 metres) and the monument is visited by people from all over the world. President Lincoln isn't too happy – he says the tourists keep getting up his nose.

WE'LL ESTABLISH BASE CAMP ON HIS CHIN AND MAKE THE ASCENT UP THE NORTH FACE!

Answer: Did you spot the deliberately false and extremely silly one? It was number **3**. Easy wasn't it?

The story of Joseph Beuys and the helpful Tartars

Grease, or rather fat, became a favourite material of German artist, Jospeh Beuys (1921-1986), after it saved his life during World War Two. Joseph was in the Luftwaffe (German Air Force). During an attack on Russia his aeroplane was shot down by the enemy.

Unfortunately for Joseph, he was in the aeroplane at the time. A group of wandering Tartars (Russian nomads) found him and his plane lying badly damaged in the snow.

The Tartars ignored the plane but took Joseph back to their tents and covered him with animal fat then wrapped him in felt in order to heal his wounds and protect him from the cold. Apart from making him really smelly, this turned out to be a very sensible thing to do. Joseph survived and was nursed back to health by his rescuers.

When he was eventually well enough to go home, and he'd said, "Ta-ta!" to the Tartars, he returned to Germany, where he became a world famous artist (not straightaway though). In later life, memories of this experience gave him the idea of using some of the things that had saved his life as part of his artwork. He made lots of sculptures out of fat and felt. He gave these works names like *Chair With Fat, Fat Corner* and *Fat Corner With Bicycle Pumps* because they were made from things like ... a chair with fat ... and fat in a corner ... with bicycle pumps!

WARNING

DO NOT SMEAR ANIMAL FAT ALL OVER YOURSELF, EVEN IF THE HEAD TEACHER HAS SWITCHED OFF THE CENTRAL HEATING TO SAVE MONEY. THE STAINS ARE TERRIBLE TO GET OUT OF CLOTHES...

Joseph sometimes slept standing up. This was because he had been wounded a total of five times during the war and his body was full of painful shrapnel. It was also badly scarred and he probably wasn't too keen on displaying it as part of his art ... unlike some other artists...

Making an exhibition of themselves

Many artists are so inspired by the human body that they use it as the raw material for their work.

Sometimes they use their own body and sometimes they use someone else's ... and sometimes they get into trouble.

1 The American artist, Jasper Johns (1930-), made casts from some of the most private bits of his body, which he then displayed to the public at art exhibitions. The casts, that is – not the real bits! He incorporated the colourful replicas of his little bits and pieces into pictures like *Target With Plaster Casts*, painted in 1955.

2 In 1994 a young woman artist took off all of her clothes and covered herself in melted chocolate. When the chocolate had set she had a perfect cast of the shape of her body. She exhibited this chocolate cast as part of the show she put on to get a University Degree. During the show, a hungry visitor ate her elbow!

MMM... NOT BAD... BUT DO YOU HAVE ANY WITH SOFT CENTRES?

3 In 1995 a female art student in Cambridgeshire wanted to make a cast of a male nude. She asked a friend if he would be the model and, when he said yes, she covered him from head to toe in plaster. Unfortunately she used the wrong type of plaster! It should have been plaster of Paris, but she used the kind of plaster that builders put on the inside walls of houses and, when she tried to break the cast, it wouldn't come off! It had set hard and the poor bloke was in agony.

The artist called the Fire Brigade who rushed the "statue" to Addenbrooke's hospital in Cambridge.

HAVE YOU NOTICED THE WAY THE EYES SEEM TO FOLLOW YOU AROUND THE WAITING ROOM?

After the bloke had been given a pain-killer his rescuers set about freeing him by chipping away the plaster with hammers and chisels. Fortunately for him, he was still wearing his socks and underpants.

4 The French artist, Yves Klein (1928-1962) seemed a bit confused about how to paint nudes. In 1961, after his young women models had taken off their clothes, he painted them all over in blue paint! When they were well and truly covered he got them to press their bodies against his canvases. It sounds a bit like doing potato prints, doesn't it, except Yves used nude women ... instead of nude spuds. Apparently the paintings made a really big impression ... and so did the women.

5 The Lebanese artist, Mona Hatoum (1952-), decided that art lovers might like an opportunity to get to know her little "ins and outs" a bit better – so she got some surgeons to make a film of the inner workings of her body ... but not with a normal video camera! The clever surgeons did the whole job with a very tiny remote-controlled camera that had been developed for use in micro-surgery. Mona was so thrilled with the final film that she had it projected onto the floor of the Tate Art Gallery as her entry for the 1995 Turner Prize art competition.

6 The British artists, Gilbert and George, quite often use themselves as their own material. They are what is known as "living sculptures" and they just ... stand around. Sometimes, if they're feeling really energetic, they move about a bit. In 1971 they made a complete exhibition of themselves at a New York art gallery by covering their faces in vaseline and shiny bronze powder and making jerky, robot like movements to the well-known song, *Underneath the Arches*.

You never know, you might have a living sculpture in your own school. It could be worth a fortune!

HEY! THAT'S NOT A LIVING SCULPTURE! MR PERKINS ALWAYS STANDS LIKE THAT WHEN HE'S ON PLAYGROUND DUTY!

Sometimes Gilbert and George display hair or ash from their cigarettes in galleries as part of an "exhibit". It's a wonder these precious art objects don't get thrown away – they're the kind of thing that tidy people would just sweep under the carpet. In the world of art it really is hard to tell the difference between rubbish ... and rubbish?

"Skip the Art, Charlie! We've got a gallery to clean!"

Michael Landy does "installations". He'd be a bit offended if you asked him to install your new gas cooker or central heating system though – Michael is an artist who makes creative "installations" of objects in galleries. Art lovers look at the objects and say things like, "These ... err ... art thingies ... are really, err ... arty ... aren't they?" But office cleaners just say, "It's a load of rubbish!" and dump the lot in a skip.

That's exactly what happened when the cleaners came across one of Michael's exciting new works. It's not surprising really. The "installation" was a bin full of rubbish – and the cleaners were only doing their job, weren't they?

This isn't the first time this has happened. The problem of cleaners throwing away bits of art because they think it's rubbish has become so common that some galleries now have to label things as either "art" or "rubbish".

So that answers one of the questions at the start of the chapter doesn't it? If you want to be sure that something is actually art, you look at the label!

169

ART   **RUBBISH**

 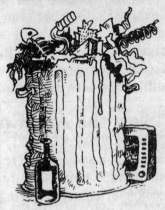

Orlan – the changing face of modern art

If gallery-goers thought that Michael Landy's ideas about art and rubbish were a bit adventurous and offbeat (outLandyish?) who knows what they would make of the Paris-based French artist, Orlan (1947-) and her ideas about art ... and plastic surgery!

WARNING
DO NOT READ IF YOU ARE OF A SQUEAMISH DISPOSITION...OR HAVE JUST HAD YOUR TEA!

Orlan, is a sort of sculptress ... but she doesn't waste hours hacking away at boring old stuff like huge chunks of marble or granite – that's for wimps! Orlan hacks away at her own face, or to be more precise, she gets a plastic surgeon to do the hacking and carving. She just comes up with the ideas – and the face. Whenever she feels artistically inspired,

170

she pops along to her friendly neighbourhood operating theatre and has a bit of her mush remodelled to match her favourite famous paintings.

Orlan's chopping list – (Orl'in the best possible taste!)

1. I'D LIKE A NEW CHIN, PLEASE. THE SAME AS THE ONE IN BOTTICELLI'S FAMOUS PAINTING OF **VENUS**. AND YOU MIGHT AS WELL GRAFT ON A NEW FOREHEAD WHILE YOU'RE AT IT... 'MONA LISA' STYLE, OF COURSE...

OF COURSE, MADAM. WILL THAT BE ALL, MADAM?

2. WELL, NOW YOU'RE ASKING... YOU COULD SLAP ON A COUPLE OF LUSCIOUS LIPS FOR GOOD MEASURE- BIG KISSY ONES, LIKE IN GUSTAVE MOREAU'S **EUROPA** PICTURE... AND, IF IT'S NOT TOO MUCH TROUBLE I QUITE FANCY MY OWN SET OF HORNS.

3. NOT AT ALL – A WISE CHOICE IF I MAY SAY SO. WHAT SORT WOULD MADAM LIKE? GOAT? COW? RHINOCEROUS? OR HOW ABOUT A PAIR OF **ANTLERS**? THEY LOOK ABSOLUTELY STAGGERING AND I HEAR THEY'RE ALL THE RAGE IN LAPLAND!

4. MMM... THEY'D BE REALLY USEFUL FOR HANGING THE WASHING ON... BUT THEN AGAIN, I DON'T WANT TO END UP LOOKING LIKE SOME SORT OF **FREAKY EXHIBITIONIST WEIRDO**, DO I? I'LL JUST SETTLE FOR A NORMAL PAIR OF HORNS. BY THE WAY, I HOPE THEY'RE NOT TOO **DEER** – I'M NOT MADE OF **DOE**!

So it's now possible to spot bits of famous paintings in Orlan's face ... and the artist's got her very own cute little set of Bambi-style horns!

She makes sure that the World of Art doesn't miss out on any of her exciting operations by having all the messy chops and changes to her face broadcast live to art galleries around the world. Lucky critics and serious art students are able to savour the sight of the surgeon's knife slicing into Orlan's flesh (quite artistically of course) and the spectacle of her blood as it squirts and spurts around the operating theatre (even more artistically). As the *ch'op*eration is actually taking place they are invited to fax suggestions about which bit she should have altered next.

If they can afford to hand over the odd £6,000 or so they can even take home a video of the whole thing – perhaps they like to watch the action replays and yell, "Cut!" at the appropriate moments?

When the job's finished nothing goes to waste – bits of Orlan (off-cut of bottom ... fillet of thigh) are collected up then carefully pickled ready to be sold to art lovers (or gourmet cannibals?). At just a few thousand pounds a portion they really are an

172

absolute snip! If you're fortunate enough (or unfortunate enough) to be a world famous celebrity and show-off, like Madonna, you won't even have to pay for your bit of the artist. She received her own personal piece of Orlan's pickled thigh as a special gift after they'd been on a TV chat show together.

How to get the most out of your art(eries)

Well, you couldn't get Awful Art more awful than Orlan's ... could you? If there was such a thing as a "Weirdometer" for measuring the sheer *awfulness* of Awful Art, then Mark Quinn's interesting, but rather grisly, little project might just send the needle spinning right off the scale! Art's in Mark Quinn's blood – and Mark Quinn's blood ... is in art! Mark's just giving an interview to Mervyn Wagg on the TV show, *Art Beat Me*. Let's listen in!

2 NINE PINTS! THAT'S MORE THAN A BUCKETFUL! DON'T YOU THINK YOU WERE BEING A BIT OVER GENEROUS? AT MY LOCAL BLOOD-DONOR'S CLINIC THEY ONLY ASK FOR A PINT.

IT WASN'T FOR THE BLOOD BANK MERV... IT WAS FOR ME ART!

3 OH RIGHT! BUT NINE PINTS IS ALMOST A WHOLE ARTIST FULL! DIDN'T THE EXPERIENCE LEAVE YOU FEELING WEAK AND DIZZY?

DON'T BE A NERD MERV! I HAD IT DONE A BIT AT A TIME!

4 OH I SEE! SO THEN WHAT DID YOU DO, MARK?

WELL MERV, YOU KNOW THAT DENTIST'S PUTTY?

5 IS HE? WHICH DENTIST IS THIS THEN, MARK?

I SAID DENTIST'S PUTTY MERVYN! THAT PLASTICKY CEMENT STUFF THEY USE TO MAKE MOULDS OF TEETH. I GOT SOME OF THAT

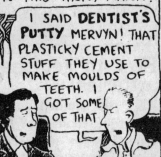

6 RIGHT, I'M WITH YOU NOW YOU WERE THINKING OF MAKING YOURSELF SOME NICE NEW GNASHERS – GOOD IDEA! SO WHAT DID YOU DO NEXT?

I PUT THE PUTTY ALL OVER MY HEAD, MERV!

7 YOU PUT IT... ALL OVER YOUR HEAD, MARK?

YUP, I MADE A MOULD OF MY HEAD WITH IT.

175

Monstrous materials two

Now that you've read about the more unusual ways in which some artists make their work you will have no difficulty whatsoever in spotting the deliberately silly and untrue one in this next selection of "monstrous materials". This one's so incredibly barmy that it stands out a mile!

1 Some chicken's eggs in incubators. German artist, Hans Haake, put these items on display in 1969. After much exhausting research and racking of his brains he gave them the inspired title of ... *Chickens Hatching* – then he probably went for a well-earned rest.

2 Lots and lots of money. A Chinese artist put his entire life savings on display in a London art gallery in 1994. Visitors to the exhibition were so impressed and excited by this work of art that they nicked the lot!

3 Three television sets and a cello player. In 1971 sculptor, Nam June Paik, made a cello out of three stacked-up television sets and some cello strings. Then he got a famous cellist to play the "cello". One of the other things that June Naim Pak did, along with some pals, was to invent the video recorder!

4 An old lady, a baseball cap and some muesli. Performance artist, Ron Rogers, exhibited his 82-year-old grandmother, Ivy, eating muesli from a Nike baseball cap at the 1988 Edinburgh Festival. He called the exhibit *Coming Of Age* and was awarded first prize for originality. (Then he gave his gran a second Alpen ... for being a good model!)

5 Three piles of burnt paper. These were exhibited by the well-known German artist, Reiner Ruthenbak. You will probably be fascinated to know that this sculpture measured 98 inches (about two metres) in length. Remember this intriguing bit of information and reveal it at an appropriate moment in an art lesson. You will no doubt be rewarded by the stunned and appreciative silence of your class-mates and teacher.

6 A stuffed goat and a tyre. These items were exhibited by American artist, Robert Rauschenberg. The stuffed goat was surrounded by the tyre. The whole thing took four years to complete, which does seem rather a long time. Then again ... it probably took him that long to stuff the goat.

7 Some bread and some spit. Sculptor, Dusan Kusmic, made a pair of miniature shoes out of bread (loafers?) mixed with his own spit. (Some people thought his work was sole'less dribble.)

8 Dew and grass. Chris Parsons of Shropshire in England gets out of bed really early so that he can dew his own thing. He uses a big brush (sweeping not painting) to make enormous abstract patterns in the moisture that has settled on people's lawns during the night.

Answer: It was **4**, but you knew that anyway didn't you? Well done! Only a complete dim-wit would have missed that one wouldn't they?

An exciting creative project to do at home on a long winter's evening

All this talk of weird and wonderful materials and the strange and often bizarre imaginations of artists, has probably left you feeling desperate to have a go at a little creative activity of your own. Here is a simple little project which you might wish to try at home in your spare time. A few of the materials are a little bit unusual, and might be quite hard to obtain. So it would probably be a good idea if you ask a grown up to help you – preferably someone famous, like the British artist, Damien Hirst. During the 1990s Damien has made a name for himself as an original and imaginative artist whose work really is at the "cutting edge" of creativity.

What you'll need
You will need the following items: some sellotape; a pair of scissors (please be very careful with these); a

really powerful chainsaw; half a dozen plastic buckets; a killer shark; two or three bin liners; a sheep; some felt-tip pens; plastic overalls; a pair of washing-up gloves; a Friesian cow; lots of old newspapers; some really strong glue (make sure it's the safe kind!); several hundred gallons of embalming fluid; step ladders; brightly-coloured sticky paper; a pair of wellington boots; and three large, glass-sided tanks. Got that? What do you mean you've changed your mind and you'd prefer to stick to painting by numbers? Don't be such a wimp! You're an artist!

All you have to do
1 Lock the front door and close all the curtains. Put on the overalls, gloves, and boots.

2 This is the easy bit. (It's a practise for the hard part which comes later.) Fill the tanks with embalming fluid and put in the shark and the sheep. No ... not together! What do you mean, "The sheep doesn't want to go in?" It's supposed to be dead! Surely you knew that?

3 Now for the main part. This isn't easy and you may need to ask for help. Having made sure that the cow is definitely the non-living variety, cut it from head to tail with the

chain saw ... so that you've got two matching halves ... no, they're not going to be book-ends! Mind your fingers! That's it, well done.

At this point you're probably beginning to realize that you've got to be so incredibly "sensitive" and "caring" if you want to be an artist. Yes, all right, it is a little bit messy! But so's finger painting! Anyway ... you put plenty of newspaper on the living-room carpet ... didn't you? Oh! You didn't! Uuurgh! Whatever is your mum going to say?!

4 This is the really tricky bit. You've got to get one half of the cow into the glass tank without any of its bits and pieces falling out. Which is where the sellotape will come in handy. Use plenty. OK. Ready steady – lift! It's fun isn't it? Just like one of those TV game shows really. You've dropped *what*? Well ... pick it up and stick it back in! What do you mean, you can't remember where it goes? All right, put it in the bin liner then!

5 What's next? Well ... nothing really. That's it, half a cow in a tank of smelly liquid ... your very own masterpiece! All you've got to do now is to make a little label with the coloured paper and felt tips and think of a title. How about *It Only Took Me Half a Moo*, or *Where's the Udder Half*? Your family will be lost for words when they see how clever you've been. They might even want to keep your creation. If they don't, why not take it down to the Tate Gallery in London and offer it to them. That's what Damien did with

180

his and they gave him £20,000! If you want to find out how Damien soared (sawed?) to stardom ... read on!

Dynamic Damien-Data

- In 1989, the not very well-known-at-all-artist, Damien Hirst (1965-), put lots of bottles of medicines and pills in a cupboard. He then called the cupboard *My Way* and put it on display at the *New Contemporaries* exhibition in London. The well-known art collector, Charles Saatchi, paid him thousands of pounds for it. Why didn't he just go to the chemist – they're cheaper?

COR! MY MUM'S GOT ONE OF THEM IN THE BATHROOM!

ONLY £10,000

- In 1990, Damien put lots of bluebottles and some rotting meat in a large glass case. The bluebottles flew around, got to know each other, laid eggs and generally had lots of fun. They were then frazzled to death on an insectorcutor (sort of electric chair for naughty flies). This "installation", which Damien called, *A Thousand Years*, was bought by the well-known art collector, Charles Saatchi, for £30,000. He obviously got a real buzz out of it! Meanwhile, Damien laughed all the way to the (bluebottle) bank.

- In 1992, Damien put a 14-foot-long tiger shark (not undead) in a perspex case full of embalming fluid and named it *The Physical Impossibility Of Death In The Mind Of Someone Living* (why not just *Joey* or *Jaws*?). The well-known art collector, Charles Saatchi, paid Damien £55,000 for it.

- Damien pickled a sheep and called it *Away From The Flock*. The well-known art collector, Charles Saatchi, bought it from him for £25,000.
- In 1995, Damien put half a cow in a case full of embalming fluid, and half a calf in a case full of embalming fluid. He entered them both in the Turner Prize art competition at the Tate Gallery ... and won.

- As he was being handed the prize winner's cheque Damien said, "It's amazing what you can do with an 'E' in A-level art, a twisted imagination and a chainsaw."

Finshing touches

After reading this chapter you might still be a bit confused about how to recognize what is actually genuine art and what is actually just a huge practical joke that is being played on the public by an artful trickster. You may also still be wondering how to tell the difference between good art and bad art. Well, why not ignore the labels and the "artrage" that often accompanies anything that is "new" or "different" and make your mind up for yourself. If you actually like a piece of art or if you find it stimulating in any way then, for you, that is good art. If you come across something which you think is awful that doesn't necessarily mean that it's not art or it's bad art. Someone else may think it's marvellous, and therefore that is good art for them. Remember – one person's *Mona Lisa* is another person's ... new forehead?

Art-searching – find art for yourself!
Jackson Pollock – *No. 27* – Whitney Museum of American Art – New York
Nam June Paik – *TV Buddha* – Stedeljik Museum, Amsterdam, Holland
Jasper Johns – *Zero Through Nine* – 1961 – The Tate Gallery, London
Robert Rauschenberg – *Retroactive* – 1964 – Wadsworth Atheneum, Hartford, Connecticut, USA
Ditto – *Monogram* (the goat one!) – Moderna Museet, Stockholm, Sweden

---

EPILOGUE

When the Prehistoric cave painters made their first pictures they had no idea that they were making works of art. Those first artists were probably doing something that came to them as naturally and automatically as going to the loo ... or running away from a sabre-toothed tiger. And when the skilled artisans of ancient civilizations were creating beautiful and elaborate decorations for temples and tombs they probably didn't know that they were making art either – they were just using their natural talents and doing the job that they'd been told to get on with.

Since those far-off times we've done something else that comes naturally – we've given all this natural creative activity a name – we've called it **art**. So, now that we all know *exactly* what we're all talking about, it's all ridiculously simple and straightforward ... isn't it? Well ... perhaps not. Art is an awfully small name for an awfully big subject – so big, that it would be completely impossible to fit it all into one book – which is one of the reasons why this one has mainly concentrated on just a few areas of European art ... and has so rudely ignored the rest of the world (sorry, rest of the world – no offence intended).

No matter where art takes place you can be sure that it will mean an *awful* lot of different things to an *awful* lot of different people. Some people want their art to be *awfully* challenging and upsetting and disturbing, so that it shocks us all into rethinking some of our more boring and cosy ideas about the world around us.

And other people want art to be *awfully* picturesque, and cosy, and heart-warming – so that it reassures and comforts them about the world around them.

Thank goodness artists don't all agree about what art should be. If they did, it would all be awfully similar and awfully boring, wouldn't it?

To Joseph Beuys, art was often just a disturbing thought or idea, expressed as a series of actions, or an arrangement of objects, which were designed to make people sit up and take notice of the general weirdness of our world. Henri Matisse preferred his public to sit down and take pleasure in the shape and form and colour of the world around them. He painted vivid, lively and cheerful pictures and said, "Art should be like a comfortable armchair." He probably wouldn't have found Joseph's *Chair With Fat* in the least bit relaxing! So, perhaps art should be whatever we want it to be?

- To you, it may well be something that you now will avoid for all time (after reading this book?). Then again ... it may be something that may well give you lots of pleasure and interest for the rest of your life?
- To your teacher, art might just be that "not quite as important as all the other subjects" school subject, that's always left until last thing on Friday afternoons (but let's hope not!).
- To fans of Carl André, Mark Quinn and Orlan, art is quite likely to be a heap of housebricks or a head made from frozen blood.
- If you're an admirer of Vermeer, art could well be an oil painting of a 17th-century woman playing an instrument as the light from a stained-glass window picks out the lovely detail of her richly textured dress.
- And to people like Vincent Van Gogh, Mona Hatoum, Stanley Spencer and all the rest (maybe even you as well?) art definitely means a Way of Life – something that's programmed into the

hard disc of their brains – something that they just can't help doing – which may occasionally send them slightly doolally ... or earn them the disapproval of other people ... or an awful lot of fame and fortune?

The Knowledge

Potty Politics by Terry Deary
Read the truth about potty prime ministers,
loony lords, vile voters, mad manifestos, crazy
canvassing ... and much more, including
exactly what it takes to be an MP.
Politics – it's potty!

Foul Football by Michael Coleman
This kickin' guide tackles everything you
need to know ... from mean managers and
rotten refs to top teams, faithful fans and all
the cracking competitions, including events
at wonder-foul Wembly!

Murderous Maths by Kjartan Poskitt
Meet One Finger Jimmy, Chainsaw Charlie
and their ghastly gangster friends, who are
living proof that maths really can be
murderous. It really is dead funny, dead
interesting, and best of all, it's got
NO NASTY EXERCISES AND NO
BORING SUMS!

The Knowledge

The Gobsmacking Galaxy
by Kjartan Poskitt
Jump up and down with excitement as you're
whisked away on a grand tour of the solar
system, where you'll go skiing on Mars and
meet the sad creature from Pluto. Plus ...
find out what happens when a bloke called
Sid gets too close to a black hole.

Groovy Movies **by Martin Oliver**
Go behind the scenes with this star-studded
guide – meet anxious actors, dastardly
directors, get animated with an A-Z of
cartoon capers, and see if the groovy movie
screen test sets you on the road to stardom.

If you want to be in the know, get
The Knowledge!